GULF COAST COMMUNITY COLLEGE
LIBRARY
5230 West Hwy. 98
Panama City, Florida

D1770039

ETHICAL LEADERSHIP OF ROBERT E. LEE

Ethical Leadership of Robert E. Lee

By Michael Lipsey

with Rusty Fischer and Susie Mercer

PELICAN PUBLISHING COMPANY
Gretna 2004

Copyright © 2001
By Michael J. Lipsey
All rights reserved

First edition, 2001
First Pelican edition, 2004

The word "Pelican" and the depiction of a pelican are trademarks of Pelican Publishing Company, Inc., and are registered in the U.S. Patent and Trademark Office.

ISBN: 1-58980-195-4

Printed in the United States of America
Published by Pelican Publishing Company, Inc.
1000 Burmaster Street, Gretna, Louisiana 70053

To my Lady and three Knights

Contents

Pride 19
Etiquette 21
Directness 24
Presence 27
Courtesy 30
Self Control 32
Fortitude 34
Forgiveness 36
Innovation 38
Gratitude 40
Patience 43
Knowledge 46
Risk 48
Strategy/Planning 51
Duty 54
Honor 57
Loyalty 60
Moderation 63
Tenacity 66

Acceptance	69
Courage	72
Obedience	75
Self Denial	78
Industry	81
Encouragement	84
Leadership	86
Reflection	88
Family	90
Order	93
Humor	96
Tolerance	98
Responsibility	101
Example	104
Compassion	106
Overconfidence	109
Discipline	111
Delegation	114
Diplomacy	117
Temptation	119
Humility	121
Chivalry	124
Faith	127
Optimism	130
Epilogue: The Final Lesson	132

Prologue

Jase Morgan was a man used to getting his own way. In his supercharged, high-powered world, delays were unheard of, deadlines were met, and failure was never an option. He sailed through daily business meetings like a well-oiled money machine, offering up inventive solutions that saved his company hundreds of thousands of dollars and avoiding problems that could have cost it millions! His unprecedented expertise in the ever-evolving world of real estate consulting was unmatched, and as such, his rewards were great.

Driving up to his towering office building each morning, he eased his luxury sedan into a reserved parking space. Security guards and office staff alike greeted him respectfully, and his coffee, mail, and messages awaited him the moment he strode into his luxurious corner office for yet another day of wheeling and dealing in properties that bore mind-boggling price tags. His calls were screened, his meetings were scheduled, and his airline tickets were pre-ordered and prepaid.

Yet now, stranded in yet another airport while watching garishly made-up flight attendants chatting aimlessly and a lethargic ground crew standing below in useless clumps, all Jase could think of was the futility of it all. "What good is being a power broker?" he thought disgustedly, "if I can't even get off the ground on time?" Jase watched as the impatient and frumpy future passengers who dotted the crowded airline terminal alternately fumed and groaned in disgust. For the third time, a now embarrassed customer service representative from the airline carrier announced that yet another delay would set their original flight departure time back by more than two hours. Yet there was no apology made, no discount fare was mentioned, not even the token gesture of free sodas or snacks was offered. Just a curt, yet threatening, "thank you for your continued patience" and then an unexpected squeak as the microphone turned off. "What a good customer-care course couldn't do for these idiots," Jase mused from his vantage point in the corner of the crowded terminal. "Why, they've given up any pretense of caring," he thought, not realizing the irony of his indignation. "I should have Tom Young in sales call the president of the airline. Our consulting company could do wonders here. Of course, so could a 5-year-old who remembered to say 'please' and 'thank you'..." Shaking his head, Jase returned his attention to the growing numbness in his lower extremities. He didn't realize it, yet he was the very picture of an overtaxed business traveler: well-tailored suit creased, tie loose and slightly crooked, his eyes ringed with circles not quite hidden beneath an unhealthy pallor from too much time on the road. Restless. Grumpy. Bored. Had they been casting for an Alka-Seltzer, Tums, or Pepto-Bismol commercial, the disgusted look on Jase's rumpled face would have made him the poster boy for such remedies.

Jase dragged a hand though his salt-and-pepper hair to no good effect, then looked at his expensive watch for the hundredth time. Only a few hours earlier, Jase had experienced unmitigated success in a boardroom halfway across the country from his family and firm. He, Jase Morgan, had leased the largest parcel in his firm's already successful history: 550,000 square feet of prime office space in Boston, none other than the seventh most expensive city on a per square foot basis in the world. He had pulled together a cushy deal for the landlord, throwing in resourceful initiatives and new revenue streams—valet parking, on-site dry cleaning, and data center maintenance—that netted him $2 per square foot over market value. It translated into better than $500,000 in additional monthly revenue. The phrase "feather in his cap" hardly began to describe what had happened mere hours ago, but now the glory had started to fade. In fact, Jase suddenly realized that he was no longer even excited about closing the deal. As was the custom in his early days as a real estate consultant, there was no adrenaline, no rush, no sense of the conquering hero returning home with the spoils of war. He had worked late for months, but for what? As soon as the ink was dry on this deal, there were three more awaiting his immediate attention! Where was the thrill in that? He was suddenly struck by the appropriateness of the term "rat race."

Next to him, a frazzled mother tried to divide her attention between three screaming brats. One of them, the youngest, had been crying nonstop for the last twenty minutes.

"What I wouldn't give for earplugs," Jase thought sullenly as the child's mother tried in vain to soothe her sobbing infant. There was a time when Jase would have felt empathy for the young mother, or perhaps even tried to amuse the baby with his shiny watch or pocket full of breath mints, keys, and other bits and bobs. God knew he'd been in that situation many a night with his own three children. Yet now he just wished she would remove the screaming nuisance from earshot. It was an impatience just below the surface. A bubbling simmer that caused him to barely hide the disgust he felt from passing across his otherwise impassive face. Back home, at the inner sanctum of his towering office, one quick word from his mouth would send a well-healed assistant to escort this woman and her three brats out into the reception area so that he could concentrate on what was really important: The next deal. Anger boiled up in his craw and he yearned to tell this frazzled woman, not to mention the rest of the whining, sniveling fools surrounding him, just what he thought of them all. He felt like that often, lately. Too often . . .

Common courtesy had prevented Jase from getting up to sit elsewhere when this young woman appeared, loaded down with children, diapers, strollers, and bags like a pack mule. Now that the flight was so late, his seating options were limited to the elderly gentleman with the persistent cough three rows over, or seats in the midst of what could only be a group of gaggling, leggy high school cheerleaders. Jase understood that he had no other recourse but to stomp to the desk and share his irritation with the closest airline representative. What was taking this flight so long? Didn't they realize he still had work to do once he got home? After all, a deal like the one he'd secured today merely meant more paperwork for him.

He leaned over awkwardly, trying to wrench his briefcase from under his seat. Biting back a curse, he freed the case, straightened himself, and immediately tripped over a child's toy as he headed up the aisle to the desk. It was all he could do not to punt the furry thing across the airport. Forty-five endless minutes later, Jase finally found himself slumping into an oversized seat in first class. He sighed ponderously, grimaced threateningly, and opened the latest issue of Commercial Property News, eager to get in the air and arrive home.

"Two hours and 45 minutes late," he thought to himself, barking his order for another scotch and soda from his leather seat. "It'll be after eleven by the time I pick up my bags, get the car, and get on the road. If I'm lucky I can be home before midnight—I guess I can see everyone tomorrow at dinner.

"No, Molly will take Jordan to football practice, and Julie has volleyball at the sports complex. John has SAT prep at the university and then will be working at Subway until late. I fly out again the morning after for ten days in London so I can tour properties..."

Despite the ferocity of his nature, his killer instincts, and the fact that he would never, ever admit it to another living soul, Jase suddenly realized that he was getting too old for this . . .

Miraculously, the seat next to him remained empty as the plane finally took off. Jase downed his scotch and soda angrily, promptly ordered another one, chose between yet another unappetizing serving of steak or fish for the sixth time that month alone, and reopened his trade magazine. "Hotel Sales Expected to Stay Steady Despite Economy." "Revamp Shops to Boost Growth Opportunities." "Optimists Say Online Lending will Succeed." Headlines flashed in Jase's head as he turned the pages, finding nothing of interest in a publication that had been his guidepost for years. He threw the paper down and rubbed his eyes.

Jase's drink arrived as he was rummaging sourly through

the airline's selection of reading materials. "Just put it down," he snapped when the flight attendant tried to hand it to him.

"*Sky Mall. Better Homes and Gardens. Sports Illustrated. Parenting Today.* Isn't there anything worth reading around here?" he asked, not intending to speak aloud. Heads turned, then swiveled politely away, as Jase's anger got the best of him and he jammed both hands into the seat pocket in front of him and yanked out its unwieldy contents. He grimaced at the subsequent ripping sound.

"What the—?" Jase blurted, though more quietly this time. Hidden behind the stack of magazines, catalogs, and flight instructions was a small book, now nearly coverless thanks to Jase's rough hands. Fascinated, he separated the worn book from the pile, absently putting the rest aside. He took a moment to adjust the cover and pages, which were loose and tattered, then set his treasure down gently. Jase stared at the ancient little book. *Daily Reflections* could barely be discerned in fading gold leaflet on the battered cover. Unable to help himself, he turned gingerly to the first page. A handwritten inscription was scribbled there:

Dear Reader.

The papers herein were not meant for publication. They were the private thoughts of a great man, written for his own edification. A man who always led by example, never by instruction. Upon his death they fell to me, a keepsake from a departed friend.

I share them with you now.

The man of whom I speak was the hero of his day, though never by his own admission. His life was a testament to humility, to honor, to duty, to faith. After his death, I was able to take great comfort in his words, and in reading them, I found myself changed—immeasurably. It is my sincerest hope that you are but a carefree soul, treaspassing here for a monent's diversion. But if you, as I did, need direction—if you are seeking answers—then by all means proceed with an open heart and a willing mind.

For you hold in your hand a treasure whose value can only be priced by your actions. You possess it now only because honor deemed that such bounty be passed on to others, as it was passed to me: without specific intention to teach, but undoubtedly with the power to change the world.

The author's signature was illegible, but Jase didn't notice. He had already turned the page . . .

Ethical Leadership of Robert E. Lee

Pride

While strolling through the streets of my hometown on a quiet afternoon, I was asked by a woman the reason for my apparently odd attire. Though circumstances have humbled me more so than in former years, and my chest of drawers contains less formal wear than years gone by, my answer was nonetheless the same: Pride.

For it is with pride that I wear the uniform of my former military days, and pride with which I hold my head up high as I wander the streets of my town in such attire. Though stripped of any insignia and rank, for fear of inciting more hatred and violence, is not the material still sturdy and the cut still flattering? Why should a man deny his years of service by purchasing a new suit he can ill afford, when that which is still upon his back is so comfortable, yet even more comforting?

Can he not regard the cut of his sleeve or the crease of his trousers and reflect upon the glory of his accomplishments and the splendor of his past? Must he deny the suit of clothes for which he paid so dearly to attain? Can he not out of respect for the accomplishments of those fallen dead, and his own, wear his suit of clothes with pride and honor all the rest of his days?

Fearing the poor woman would reel with the heady formality of such a complicated reply, I simply regarded her kindly and spoke but a few words: "It is with pride, madam, that I wear the suit of clothes awarded to me by my years of faithful service, much as a doctor wears his cloak or a priest must wear his robe. Would you deny an old soldier his uniform, and with the same decree deny that for which he fought so fiercely?"

Considering my answer, she fingered my sleeve and commented upon its material, still so firm and sound months after it was issued to me. Apparently satisfied by its cut, not to mention my answer, she went on her way without further comment, leaving me to ponder today's reflection.

For if I'd been ashamed of my actions, the suit upon my back would be anathema to me and those of my kin. But with pride I adorn it, and with pride I wear it, and with pride I must amble through the length of my days.

And so, I would hope, would you have pride in past accomplishments and thus trumpet your own horn before those around you would squelch such a harmonious sound. Though vanity remains a sin, pride in proper doses is medicine for the businessman's soul, and salve for his ego on days when the tide has turned and his fortunes reversed. Let not your pride be wounded, lest your heart still bear the scars.

Etiquette

Because of deeds both real and imagined during my public life, I receive parcels of mail each day. Letters come from far and wide, from friend and foe, from the youthful and the young at heart. Some want nothing more than to congratulate me on my accomplishments, real or perceived. Others are soliciting quotes for books, or my help in obtaining monetary funding for some idealistic project or another. Some are hurtful, others bring tears of pride or joy to my eyes. Old friends write to rekindle relationships, and young women write to begin new ones.

And despite my heavy workload as a college president, despite my advancing age and ill health, I find time to answer each and every piece of correspondence I receive. From friend and foe, from young and old, from near and far, I sit at my desk and compose thoughtful replies to difficult questions. Business etiquette demands it, and did it not my own, personal etiquette would surely require as much!

Though they are offered with a generous appeal, I use no signature stamps or form letters, no secretary or assistant. I reply thoughtfully to each and every piece of correspondence, by hand, every single day of my working life.

Why does such a busy man answer all his own mail? The answer came to me in a letter this very day. A young boy had written to tell me of his father's feelings. His father, you see, had been one of my soldiers in a long-ago war. This boy related touchingly how his father had written home on many a night, speaking proudly of battles we'd won together. The father spoke of how I'd inspired him to be more brave and courageous than his own nature would have allowed, through some kind word of encouragement or small sign of common decency. The boy included the last letter his father ever composed, before being killed in battle the very next day. In it were fond words for the boy, yet even fonder words for myself.

I treasure that letter, and will keep it near to my heart until the end of my own days. Yet I would never have read it should I have passed off my letter-writing duties to some assistant or clerk. Many of my contemporaries consider it Lessons From the "acceptable" to go without responding to one's personal correspondence. To assign such an onerous duty to one's assistant or secretary, or to send out form letters in reply to personal messages from friends and foes alike, is quite the measure of the day.

But avoid the simple alternative and adhere to an etiquette that seems to be forgotten these days. Why buy that lightweight novel when you can spend the time instead reading messages that may improve your business—not to mention your life? How many tips or ideas do you miss each day as you carelessly toss letters in the waste bin or assign them to inexperienced or hurried assistants?

Take care that in your efforts to lighten your load, you don't also ruin your business! After all, what life altering message might you have read today, had you only opened your own mail?

Directness

I was reminded today of the frivolity of language, and the verbosity of those who find themselves more interesting than do their audience! For with the rise of power comes position, and with position comes authority, and with authority comes the unattractive feature of a man who loves to hear himself talk. God forbid I should ever join the ranks of such pompous characters in their search for one hundred words to convey the meaning of but one!

Upon this grievous morn I received a reply from a grave letter I felt forced to write only days earlier. As the general of a defeated force, I had offered my letter of resignation after one of the largest military losses ever handed to a leader of my former stature. Brought low by the enemy forces and facing a battlefield strewn with victims of my incompetence, I had drafted the letter to my President.

Humble in tone, yet forceful in language, the letter spoke of my ailing health and ineptitude on the field of battle, as evidenced by the day's resounding defeat at the hand of the enemy, or perhaps even due to my own inexperience. As I prepared myself to the matters at hand, collecting my papers and gathering my things, I was reminded of my previous communications with this President. Both of us men of few words, our brevity was matched only by our directness.

When he gave an order, to a letter it was followed by myself. Were I to disagree, my words of directness were listened to and acknowledged in turn. In words carefully chosen, phrases fully thought out, our sentiments were shared through open mouths or messages by courier, and if more men shared our directness, the world would be surely lacking in hot air!

This President's reply to my letter of resignation, received earlier today, was no different. To each of my points for resignation, he provided ample counterpoints. To each insistence, he replied with conviction in the opposition. In the end, he replied with sincerity to my insistence upon being relieved of my duty and reassigned to a position of less authority so that the troops could be led by a more able leader: "...to ask me to substitute you by someone in my judgment more fit to command, or who would possess more of the confidence of the army, or of the reflecting men of the country, is to demand an impossibility."

And with those words, he returned my sense of dignity, faith, and honor, to himself be rewarded with a chagrined leader now resolved to lose no further ground to the advancing troops of the enemy.

Therefore, be not full of verbiage or useless words. Say what you mean, and mean what you say, so that listeners will not yawn with boredom or roll their eyes in disdain, but instead be inspired by your directness and walk away assured of your wants, needs, and desires. In this way will both of you be rewarded with success in all matters.

Presence

When reflecting upon today's grim events, I am astounded not only by the viciousness of men, but by their compassion as well. After all, were it not for this latter trait of my fellow mortals, my actions would have fallen on deaf ears and I might have met as unpleasant a fate as the man I rescued!

It began with a legal transgression, either real or imagined, and a man being arrested and incarcerated for his alleged crime. As news of the accused man's capture spread throughout the community, his misdeeds grew in direct proportion to the distance such news traveled, and in record time an entire town was convinced of his guilt, without the benefit, dare I say the inconvenience, of a trial.

As the man was led through the streets from his holding cell to the courthouse, an angry mob grew convinced that justice would be denied were he to set foot inside the hallowed halls of law. Determined to bring a swift and fitting end to the man's crimes, not to mention his very life, the milling mob bestowed upon itself the lofty titles of judge, jury, and executioner!

Stringing up a noose from a sturdy tree, the bloodthirsty

crowd called for justice, nay revenge, and planned to settle accounts without benefit of anything even resembling a fair trial. Not one to condone such criminal acts, either by a guilty individual or an angry mob, I was determined that this man should go to court and be proffered his rights to a fair and speedy trial in front of a jury of his peers. After all, had I not just fought a brutal and bloody battle to defend those rights bestowed upon us by the very constitution of our beleaguered country?

Thus hearing the mob, I hastily left my chores to see what could be done. Fortunately, as I approached the unruly melee, my status and prestige in the community preceded me. Though my anger was aroused at this unlawful gathering and its evil intent, duty required me to remain calm as the crowd slowly parted to let me advance to its head. Speaking slowly and carefully so that my words would not be misconstrued for those of riotous intent, I tried to sway the crowd from its unquenchable ire.

Apparently, it worked. Through a dignified presence and calm appearance, my ministrations soothed the savage beasts and thus led them to part company without parting an unfortunate victim—from his life! Though I alone could not prove this man's guilt or innocence, neither could an unqualified crowd such as this, no matter how loud or ravenous they appeared.

Let his fate be sealed by a court of law, as wiser heads prevail and emotions no longer play a part.

Heed too, this lesson of making of yourself a calm presence

in turbulent times. Let not needless anger spew from your lips or frenzy escape your visage. May your countenance be the very picture of serenity in times of trouble, to soothe those around you, be they superiors or peers. Yours will be the counsel they seek, as your very presence has led them to the conclusion that you are a wise and gentle soul, keen on proving righteousness and truth.

Courtesy

It was with great hope that I today made a solemn vow: If I can make gentlemen of the boys in my charge, I shall count my days on earth well spent. For there is no higher calling than to be the soul of courtesy when passions might dictate otherwise.

The simplest place to impart these lessons is with the ladies, for what man cannot find it within himself to put on a charming face to please a member of the fairer sex? Young or old, plain or fair, when women are present young gentlemen should feel their courtesy rising up in them as sap in a young tree.

Sometimes, however, examples must be set. As so occurred recently when I was vacationing with my family at a popular resort. Apparently, tensions were still running high surrounding the all-too-recent conflict. A divisive attitude had begun to prevail. Sides were being taken, courtesy thus dashed with the wind. Spying an opportunity to make amends, I crossed the room and requested the hand of a young lady sitting alone, asking that I might escort her to the ballroom. "I would be honored. Sir," was her demure reply. To which I countered, "The honor is entirely mine." And so it was.

It mattered not in the least to what "side" she belonged. Of grave import was that a courtesy had been neglected, which translated to a duty being left undone. We all owe a sacred duty of hospitality to our guests, whether in our homes or merely on our soil.

And so here is the treatise I have hit upon after much reflection: It matters not the bank account nor prestige of a man, but instead judge him on his courtesy to others. For no mortal is above common decency, no man so low they cannot be helped up with an outstretched hand or warm heart.

And so shall it rest with you: Fear not the common courtesy that rests within your heart, for to show compassion is not considered weakness—but indeed the test of a true man.

Self Control

It is with a heavy heart that I compose today's reflection, upon which I have spent many an hour in careful consideration before pen was ever put to paper. For it was with regret that I today surrendered my weary troops to the enemy, and though saving their lives in the process, sealed forever their fate as well.

But consider my dilemma, and heed its tale: For with our forces outnumbered and outgunned, outsmarted and outmanned, what choice was left for me to consider? Surely, my men could have retreated and rested to fight another day. But with the enemy surrounding us and pounding us with every skirmish, would their exhaustive efforts have mounted to little more than an exercise in futility?

On the other hand, I could have allowed the men to retreat before they would be captured, casting their fates to the wind and letting them run free across the land of the enemy to hopefully return to their homeland, their lives in tact. While they might have retained their pride, had they lived, consider the innocent victims they might have encountered upon the way.

Would these rough and savage men, so long under the

firm reigns of my control, allow their base desires to come upon them while sneaking through the countryside unencumbered by a leader's good graces, not to mention his good sense? What revenge would they seek on the enemy's conspirators, should they come across one or more in a chance and violent encounter? What havoc would they wreak upon the enemy's farmland, setting fire to crops and torching homes along the way? What innocent victims would fall prey to their wrath should they happen to be in the wrong place at the wrong time?

Yet a surrender would allow the men to return home not as prisoners, or even as soldiers, but as veterans of a war which they had lost, but lost valiantly and in spite of their actions, not because of them. Wouldn't this be enough to salve their wounded egos and battered pride, so that they would no longer face an enemy, but a victor instead?

Furthermore think not the act of surrendering a rash decision, but consider instead the hours of self-control spent pondering the many solutions, both negative and positive. Were I to act hastily, lives could be lost. But with consideration, those same lives, and those of many innocent victims, could instead be saved.

Consider, then, the art of self-control in your own dealings, whether at work or at home. Let not anger lead your actions, but instead control yourself and consider all of the options before acting rashly in a manner that might do you, or even those in your employ, harm.

Control yourself, and control your fate in turn . . .

Fortitude

Like so many others have before, today's reflection came to me while sitting astride my faithful steed. For as I rode today, I was reminded of many similar journeys made not so very long ago, ones that found me passing through my beleaguered troops, dizzy from the fray, weary from the fight, bloody from the violence.

Though the war would soon be lost, and though the tide would never again turn in favor of myself or my men, I saw fortitude in the eyes of these downtrodden souls, a glimmer shining where none should have the right to gleam. For an army, many times the size of my own, full of well-fed soldiers grown strong on the meat of victory, lay ever in wait just over the next rise. I had only to ride along their lines to be sure of that grave news—and my responsibility to my men.

Yes, my men, who deserve all praise for their determination and their stout hearts. These brave souls exemplify fortitude as well as any dictionary or encyclopedia could. For my troops were the very picture of fortitude. Unshod, starving, they rallied again and again against an enemy equal to a millstone hung around the neck of a champion swimmer.

And yet they were willing to swim on in depths full leagues beyond their strongest stroke.

And yet striding among these men atop my worthy steed, I still remember cadets, not yet old enough to shave, marching through the valley of death to face the enemy. This they did despite the unkind version of "Rock-a-bye Baby," sung gaily by their older counterparts. Those boys fought so bravely, though many would die, that they silenced both their friends and their foes. Fortitude. Of the spirit, of the body.

Though battle may test the will of men, the sheer constancy of daily life can require as much fortitude as the bloodiest battle. For are not the enemies at your door? Does not the press of time wear heavy on your mind? Have not the decisions of the past come back to haunt you, again and again? Do not your accounts fluctuate with the ebb and flow of daily commerce, rising and falling like the evening tide?

Therefore fear not the whimsical nature of everyday life. But instead, know the courage in your heart and the persistence with which you have always managed to prevail. In short, do as I did: Press on.

Forgiveness

Forgiveness. It is a lost art these days, I fear. For how challenging is it to forgive someone who has wronged us so grievously, or only wronged us in some insignificant matter?

In military matters, as in life, forgiveness assumes many forms. For instance, as a battle rages on, sometimes for weeks, sometimes for months, sometimes even for years, some of the most skilled soldiers are cut down the most rapidly. The enemy targets these important and well-trained men, and eliminates them strategically, as if they themselves were targets, or merely pawns.

As the years drag on, the demand for trained military men outweighs the supply, and eventually a city, a town, or a country must call on its reserves to feed the endless machinery known as modern warfare. Many of the men who are asked to serve their country are inexperienced civilians: doctors, lawyers, writers, or tradesmen. They must learn the basic art of war in half the time of the men they are replacing. Indeed, too often are they rushed onto the battlefield with only a rudimentary knowledge of the weapon in their hands, the packs on their backs, and the desires of the enemy running at them with bloodlust in his eyes.

Occasionally, these men are put into positions of authority, whether they deserve such lofty station or not. Perhaps their education impresses a politician far from the field of battle, or perhaps they bluff their way too soon to preeminence. Either way, an inexperienced man in power can do more damage to his own army than perhaps the enemy ever could, and so it was when I found myself with a staff comprised almost entirely of new officers.

Yet not only were they new officers, but new soldiers as well. Though brave, they were inexperienced, and mistakes were often made that cost not only pivotal battles, but more importantly, the lives of good and earnest men. Yet how could I rail at these inexperienced soldiers over their costly mistakes? After all, time and circumstance had thrown all of these men together, the good with the bad, the old with the young, the inexperienced with the expert. How was I supposed to compare one man against the other, or blame the second because he'd not had the experience of the first?

Instead, upon each failure, disastrous or minor, crucial or careless, I would invite the inexperienced soldier into my tent and politely explain to him just exactly what it was he'd done wrong. Through leadership, through gentleness, but most importantly through forgiveness, these men became not only better soldiers, but better men.

With forgiveness, you too can change the lives of others, be it in your own workplace, or in the greater world at large. Forgive those who would fail you, and the likely result will be less failure for you to forgive!

Innovation

It has always been thus: Without change men stagnate, their hearts and minds fouled by the muck of outdated methods and overused ideas. But the white waters of innovation keep thinking fresh and minds clear. A man on the pond may become complacent, aware only of the pattern sunlight makes upon the water, never seeing the dangers in the depths. A man on the rapids is alert to all possibilities, knowing himself to be fully alive as each new challenge tests his resolve.

Both the pond and the rapids hold the potential for death; only one promises the potential for true life. Why then, do so many stubbornly choose the placid pond over the rushing river?

I was reminded of this ageless question today, upon the very fields of battle over which I reflect while jotting this day's tardy entry. After all, the tide of battle had turned yet again, for while my men were hearty, their numbers were insignificant when compared to that of the enemy. Still, I chanced upon an innovation I had heard about on foreign soil, and considered it for myself as I noticed the unused picks and shovels loitering from my soldiers' backs.

"Dig!" was my order, and so my men dug. Working the earth like expert farmers, they fashioned crude embattlements camouflaged to look like earthen fields and brushy hillocks. All along the terrain, this new idea unfolded like an architect's dream, while all the while my stubborn men cursed my hair-brained tactics, and begrudged my vain airs.

Yet how they did thank me when the ambush of their enemy and mine was successful, kissing their shovels and spades like long-lost sweethearts and tossing their sweat-stained caps into the air as if at a parade. Though who could begrudge their former lack of enthusiasm over such a new concept? After all, none had ever heard of any soldier worth his salt hiding behind earthworks. To them it seemed dishonorable. They begrudged the work, but many lived to thank me later.

So find it with yourself. Look not into stagnant ponds for inspiration, but ride the wildest rapids of your imagination to find innovation splashing you in the face at every turn. Though many in your employ will curse you, do not hold it against them—when they just as quickly rush to thank you!

Gratitude

My hand trembles now, impeding my writing. My heart is full, hampering my thoughts. I was honored again today, blessed once more with a reminder of the importance of gratitude. For if a man could let his life be guided by constant thankfulness, what a Utopia this would be. I know it to be true, for not two hours ago a man knocked on my door and caused me to feel once more the gentle surgery of gratitude at work in my soul, excising all unkind and base thoughts with expert hands.

Recently I was taken to task for standing up against forces I deemed to be dishonorable. After many contests and much bloodshed, I surrendered in the name of preservation—of life, of dignity, of country. Since then times have oft been difficult, with many believing they have little to live for, let alone for which to be thankful.

But daily I am reminded to see the good, to remember that a fire leaves the ground ready for new growth. This man today was such a reminder. He had come countless miles to offer me, once his commander, protection against forces he saw as massing against me. This man's clothes were tattered and worn. He was obviously of the simple folk untainted by the depredations of city life. It took great courage for him to come here, and even greater courage to speak to me. I watched his throat work as he tried to form the words, and then abruptly they burst out as if a dam had been broken.

Suddenly I knew that, even though I have tasted defeat, I can never be defeated if I can find cause to be grateful. And I am grateful. My people are vanquished, much of our lands and cities wrecked, but I find that I can still be grateful. Grateful to have served with men such as this one. Grateful that I have a home and family. Grateful for the opportunities now afforded this amazing nation of mine as we overcome adversity together.

The ability to see things in this light makes the pain of what has gone before so much easier to bear. I am blessed. Sometimes my eyes simply need to see the trees within the forest. The forest may be distressing to encompass, but each tree is remarkably easy to climb, and therein lies gratitude.

I tried to demonstrate my gratitude to this brave soul by offering him a meager, material gift in return. He was visibly shocked that I would even consider responding in such a fashion. A difficult moment ensued, one that ended only when he understood my gift as a symbol of something deeper than I could hope to express. This he accepted graciously, leaving me nearly agape at his sense of honor and duty.

Thus let gratitude be a shining beacon all the days of your life. For as the seas swell and rain falls, be grateful for a skiff to ride them out and a coat to keep you warm. Fear not the boat's untidy visage or the Jaseet's frayed collar and hem—for the reward for seeing past the waves and through the clouds will find gratitude heaped upon you in abundance. Oh, what a treasure indeed!

Patience

Reflecting yet again upon the dogs of war, it is with regret that I must admit: Impatience buried thousands of my men. It was a hooded, skeletal figure, tireless in the digging of graves. Graves that looked like hungry mouths.

Had not so many died that tombstones were too numerous to afford, countless markers would have read, "He did not wait." Even today, where I spend my days on administrative duties, the paradoxes of war continue to confound me with their exquisite multiplicity. Brash young soldiers, having drunk the heady wine of combat, will grow ever more bold, impatient for the clang of metal and scent of smoke yet again. Their bravery is to be commended, the pennies laid upon their eyes.

Somewhere in the middle of cowardice and bravery, however, lies that sturdy companion: patience.

But take care not to confuse patience with inactivity, however similar they may appear on cursory inspection. Do not doubt that one is a virtue, the other a sin. The patient man is attentive to all aspects of a situation, constantly weighing options and then carefully waiting for the precise moment to execute his designs. The inactive man waits until he is beset and then reacts as best he can.

Both kinds of men—patient and inactive—have filled those ragged, aforementioned graves, lain down next to the man of impatience. Such is the nature of war. But of those three types of men, only one ever dies unsung.

I have oft found joy in exercising patience. Thinking so, I am reminded of my little friend who visits with me in church. He sometimes climbs up on the pew next to me and lays his head upon my shoulder, looking at me with eyes trusting and enormous as I listen to the sermon. On one occasion he was privileged enough to attend the graduation ceremonies of the college where I preside. He saw me on the platform, seated while other prominent figures gave commencement speeches, so he wiggled away from his parents and sought to join me. When he attained the platform he sat at my feet, rested his little head against my knee, and promptly fell asleep. What was I to do?

I admired this boy's innocent audacity and so took the only appropriate course of action: I handed out diplomas while sitting down! The graduates were amused and the boy had his nap. Patience served us well that day, its rewards immediate. The true test comes, however, when one can use patience to achieve goals whose rewards exist only as a mere silhouette on the horizon.

So strive not to rush to action, least not where business is concerned. Where money is at risk, best to sleep on ideas that could prove costly if not implemented cautiously. Confuse not patience with inactivity, for one can be as active as a bumblebee while all the while filling his honeycomb for the long winter to come.

Patience is nothing if not tenacious, for even a pebble can start an avalanche . . .

Knowledge

It is with pride that I reflect upon today's commencement proceedings. Though it may not reflect the fanfare and hoopla of my many hard-won military victories, it is with a humble esteem that I preside over this small college and its roster of students so full of hope and enthusiasm.

For today these young boys will graduate, eventually to become men. Under my tutelage, they gained knowledge that I could never have imparted upon a battlefield. In my former life, as it were, I thought little of leading a battalion of boys no older than those just graduated today across a bloody battlefield to lose their life in the cause of freedom and justice.

And while it may have been what history demanded of me, and indeed its young men, it was far from what my heart desired for these young boys. Though with vanity I admit that once upon a time I felt my years on the battlefield the most precious of my life, it is with a great amount of humility with which I presented diplomas this very afternoon.

For in the bright and shiny faces of this nation's youth, I saw not the fear and tragedy of those of my soldiers, but the hope and promise that accompanies a young man on his way out into the world. Knowledge, therefore, is key to their success, both in business and in life.

For while my military knowledge may have brought victory to many young soldiers, the chinks in its armor brought just as much death and destruction to those in my service. Here is an opportunity to impart a different kind of knowledge, of art and of literature, of math and of science, to save our fair country from destruction, instead of bringing destruction upon its innocent youth.

And so it is with knowledge that you, too, can face a future brightened by that of hope, and not shadowed by destruction. Be your knowledge obtained through hardship or hard schooling, at your parent's knee or an instructor's booming voice, retain it all and build on it constantly. Through reading and listening will you gain more knowledge throughout your life, and use it to your advantage as each situation should dictate.

Fear not the toils of gaining knowledge, but embrace them instead—for with knowledge comes the key to success, and the number of doors it opens is limited only by yourself.

Risk

Before I began my life as an educator, I lived the violent life of an embattled general, defeating, and being defeated by, armies of great size and number, not to mention bravery and ferocity. Yet little of that brutal education prepared me for the life of a college president, or for the very real courage with which risk is undertaken on the everyday battlefield we call life. They say the pen is mightier than the sword, and from one who has wielded both, let it ring from the rooftops that I most heartily agree!

With the rise of my name came prestige and recognition, while at the same time the board of a local college found themselves in dire straits. Each year's class of students dwindled fewer than the year before, and funding became a constant impediment to the matters of educating those students who remained. Therefore, the board recently decided that one of its members would solicit me to become the president of this ailing educational institution. The philosophy was that based upon my good name alone, students would be lured to the institution. Once there, they would find halls of higher learning well worth their tuition, not to mention their time.

Nervously, the board considered their decision to approach me. Here I was, a man of apparent stature and prestige, a stern man of fierce loyalty and passion. Yet here they were, a beleaguered institution that couldn't even afford to hire me! But what they didn't know was that my years of military service, life-and-death battles, and ill health had caused me to consider a quieter life of study and reflection.

And although they had heard of me, I'd never heard of them. Therefore they had no cause to believe that a retired general would ever consider presiding over anything as "unchallenging" as a private college!

Yet they took that risk, even going so far as to borrow $50 to buy a presentable suit for the man they sent to me last week, with some leftover for his meager expenses on the journey. With no money to pay my salary, they hoped to fund my wages through the increased tuition paid by students lured to their school by my very presence within its hallowed halls.

And so it was that I met with the school's dapper looking representative, and took his offer under consideration with a stern countenance. Though they had no cause to know it, their offer appealed to me more than they could have ever surmised. Here was an opportunity to share my years of experience with the impressionable youth of our country, so recently torn apart by bloody battles. Instead of calling them to arms, I could resolve them to peace, and instruct them in the finer arts of life, such as great literature and art, math and science.

And so, after a reasonable amount of consideration, I agreed to the college's offer this very morning. Like two strangers on a chance encounter, their risky attempt to borrow money and offer me a position for which they still could not compensate me brought a meeting of the minds and resulted in a benefit to both parties.

Risk, it seems, is the only thing that brought us together. And had it not been for the risk they took, my life would have never been the same. Of that I am certain. Deny not yourself those risky schemes that keep you awake at night, for they are often the seeds of inspiration needed to sustain you come the morrow!

Strategy/ Planning

Though many come from sudden inspiration, today's reflection appears to be the result of a happy accident: A boy appeared in my office today, inquiring about entrance into the university. I do not believe he even bothered to comb his hair, which says quite a bit about the state of his clothing. I think perhaps he took a spill, or was in a fight, prior to crossing my threshold.

The young man seemed surprised to have been admitted directly to see me, for he hastily smoothed his rumpled shirt front and brushed at his dusty trousers before stammering a hesitant, "S-sir? I had not thought to see you today..."

Based on his appearance, I would gather he had thought to see the keeper of a grog shop, to perhaps inquire after a position sweeping the floor. Were I that keeper, this boy still would have gotten no work from me.

Despite his good intentions, the boy had no plan, no method set in his mind to attain his goal. He had thought to see an underling today, to test the school's waters, and then to formulate a plan at his leisure. Few have such luxury, as he found out when I sent him packing only minutes after crossing my threshold.

When I applied to military college as a young man, I was armed with no less than six letters of recommendation, all from respected men of various professions, and including one of my own stating my intentions. And I did not simply wander into the president of the college's offices; I secured an interview well in advance, leaving myself plenty of time to prepare my remarks and to study the character of the man I was to meet. Plainly, I had a plan. Now, as the president of an institution of learning myself, I am honor-bound to send such boys away, that they might think on their own improvement. How else will they win the challenging contests life has in store for them?

Some still say that I am no good example, since I was forced to offer up the white flag in my not-too-distant past. Yet I say: Within that great defeat were so many small victories—victories that were the result of strategic planning. I mastered the rails before my opponents, using them to move men and supplies and arms. I allowed my generals to break with military tradition and divide forces to flank the enemy. Outgunned and outmanned, I maneuvered around the greatest minds of our times, strategizing against the inevitable. Certainly I lost, but must those precious gains be entirely discounted?

Planning and strategy are paramount considerations when mapping out any undertaking, whether it be a family trip, a business venture, or a military campaign. If one can marshal one's forces and bring them to bear with a clear plan, success is always within reach. So fear not the calendar or notebook, and log your thoughts to victory. For it is not with rash hastiness that victories are secured, but with sustained brilliance ...

Duty

This long and burdensome day has witnessed my sense of duty put to the test, a test that I fear I may have passed at the cost of my very own sons! For as the most recent contest in my ongoing campaign of wills rages on, fresh soldiers fill my camp most night and day. Like doomed livestock, I herd them through the machinations of warfare to their fate. Some go off to battle never to return, others stagger back in the guise of war torn veterans, their scars too deep to see from the outside.

As is the case with most military campaigns, restrictions placed on which soldiers can fight under which commanders loosen as the days turn to weeks and the months turn to years. So it has transpired in this battle of wit and warfare. Today, friends fought alongside friends, brothers battled alongside brothers, and occasionally, sons campaigned under their fathers.

And so it was in this war, that I have found myself a captive of the latter category. Not one but two of my sons fought under my leadership in battles bloodier than I, or certainly they, would have preferred. Yet on this day raged out of control a battle so brutal that both of my sons participated in fierce fighting at the same time. Despite my love for them, I had no choice but to send my two children into a conflict so violent that I was quite sure that one, or possibly both, would not return. With my wife's stern face staring at me from the depths of my conscience, I wondered had I gone mad with bloodlust!

Still, my sense of duty was so strong, as was theirs, that I sent them, and did they go, quite willingly. From the sidelines I watched my forces struggle against a worthy opponent, equally matched, while the battle raged on at a disquieting level until reinforcements joined the opposing side and the tide turned for the worse. More blood was spilled and more soldiers lost as a great and valiant struggle ensued before my eyes.

Eventually, the opposing side retreated into the woods beyond the battlefield, and the troops let up a wild cheer to celebrate their victory. Upon returning to camp, bloody and ragged, tired and fearful, I was quite sure that they looked forward to a well-deserved rest after fighting off their imposing enemy.

But from my post, I was forced by duty's firm hand to issue one last edict that day. I told my men to go back into the field and find their opponent. To finish them off, unless they wanted to repeat the same battle again the next day. And the next and the next. I knew that the opposing forces were at a loss, confused and dazed, fractured and fearful.

Alternately, my force was still in one piece and filled to overflowing with the already heady rush of victory. Should they pursue and capture the enemy now, they could avoid further conflict in the future. It was my duty to order such a strategic and logical strike, and their duty to uphold the order.

My sons, upon hearing of their father's orders, came to me privately to try to dissuade me. "But father," they appealed. "Would you send us back out into the fray after such a fierce battle?"

As their father, but more importantly, their leader, I nodded and told them that, yes, I would send them back out into the fray as many times as it took to ensure victory. And so I ordered, and so they went.

Duty frequently calls. As a leader, it is often your troops who must answer the call for you. Be not afraid to let them do so, and they will respect you for it. Be not deaf to duty's call, for it resounds with a thunderous voice, which all men hear, but few men heed.

Honor

It is the classic conundrum: Each generation unto itself believes that its leaders and heroes are morally corrupt, and each generation bemoans the absence of men without moral conviction or even the faintest trace of honor. Only by living an honorable life can one combat the social and moral weakness that so pervades our society. Today, however, I learned that honor can be found in the most unlikely of locations.

This very afternoon, I stood chastised in front of a great military leader as we faced each other in the secluded corner of yet another bloody battlefield. Hundreds of men had lost their lives the previous day, and in the hopeless face of a desperate situation, I had finally admitted defeat and agreed to meet my rightful victor to discuss the terms of my egregious surrender.

While I had nothing but respect for this brilliant military leader, there was also much more at stake in our meeting of the minds. We had fought each other bravely for years, and neither the conqueror nor the conquered could afford to be hasty now. Should the victor be too generous in his terms, his soldiers and country might be disappointed and prone to act with revenge upon my defeated forces. Should I be too demanding or hostile in my terms, the victor could just as easily continue fighting and destroy my forces until the bitter end.

Naturally, we approached each other with great caution and trepidation. Bone-weary and exhausted, we shook hands and proceeded directly to the matter at hand. Hesitantly, we began discussing the terms of surrender, hateful though that word may be to the core of my soul.

Since I was the unfortunate party who was surrendering, I let my victor begin the most depressing proceedings. Slowly writing down my terms, we circled each other carefully. Eventually, it became even more evident to myself that my opponent was indeed an honorable man. More honorable, it would appear, than I had originally hoped. If I made a polite and reasonable suggestion, the victorious general quickly countered with a fair and just alternative before allowing it into the terms of surrender, without squabble or fanfare.

After a length of time, we had come to a reasonable agreement and the surrender was signed with confident yet reluctant hands. Despite the years of fiercely fought battles between us and the loss of life we had both witnessed at each other's hands, we saw eye to eye and neither blinked, nor stared coldly.

We realized that without honor, those battles, wounds, and death were meaningless. That without honor, all that we had fought for would have been for naught. That without honor, our lives, and those of our soldiers and those they had defended, were entirely meaningless.

And with honor, we who had once been bitter enemies shook hands like old friends. From this day forward, and throughout the rest of my hopefully long and productive life, this general who has lost the war yet had been treated so fairly by his victor, vows to never let an ill word be uttered about the man who had issued the terms of my surrender. With honor, I signed the treaty. And with honor, I must live with those terms forever.

And so it must be with you. Politicians will continue to disappoint, celebrities will continue to be less than inspiring, and even your family and friends will be no more perfect today than they were yesterday.

But your choice to remain honorable in the face of dishonor will give you the confidence you need to face each day anew, and to see every failure as another opportunity to learn and succeed . . .

Loyalty

Through my daily dose of much reflection, I have arrived at thus: Never have men been so loyal as those who fought with me to preserve the values and beliefs stitching together the patchwork of our way of life. Those ragtag men, so stubborn, so courageous, still have the power to move me, years after I have ceased any military command. Would that I could have served them better. Would that I could return them unharmed to their sisters and wives.

My task, then, has been no easy one, to turn that fierce loyalty down another channel. Much more challenging certainly than my earlier days spent realigning the mighty Mississippi in its course. Both endeavors, however, were for the good of a people whose situation is always at the center of my thoughts. Well worth any sacrifice I may make on my part.

The difficulty lies, then, in demonstrating the downfall of pride, even though that pride is so rightly placed. A pride I feel as sharply as they. It pains me to suggest they take up new colors that they may look to the future. How to dispel this confining hatred? It allows the victor to remain victorious, while we remain downtrodden. New loyalties must be forged.

I met a woman today, a widow of the war. Her heart was steeled against those she saw as our oppressors, and her anger and passion were clearly evident in her speech and manner. As emotional yet as the day of our surrender, she harbored such deep resentment and hatred for our victor that it was almost painful to be in her presence.

And though she looked to me for solace as a compatriot and friend, yet I felt duty bound to say to her, "Madam, do not train up your children in hostility to the government. Remember, we are all one country now. Dismiss from your mind all sectional feeling, and bring them up to be loyal. Rear them to be mindful of their leaders, and caution them against ill will or treasonous thought. This you must do to preserve our way of life, our way of honor, and our very freedom as Americans."

I can only hope that my words, and actions, will serve to twist her away from the gory scenes of what has gone before. We must sacrifice pride in the name of unity. Unity demands loyalty, painful though it may seem at the outset.

I am blessed in my current occupation, I think, to know loyalties less convoluted. In my work at the college my loyalties are far more easily given, though not more readily. Clearly I must be loyal to the task that I have set myself here, which is to continue to educate the young men of my war-torn land, who will save us from destruction with their knowledge. When others solicit me with offers of fame and wealth, or jobs with less taxing duties, I gladly answer them. My answer is always a resounding, "No, thank you."

I have a self-imposed responsibility to the young men I led in battle; I have seen many of them die on the field. I shall devote my remaining energies to training young men to do their duty in life. And so I am loyal to the university, which provides me that avenue.

So thus be loyal in your own dealings. Follow not the whims of greedy corporate leadership or mismanagement, but stay true to the larger issues of company policy and moral decency. Staying loyal to your virtues will thus inspire loyalty from those in your employ—a loyalty necessary for their success—and yours.

Moderation

I find it sometimes instructive to look back on writings from my war days. Lessons learned on the battlefield can often be applied to civilian life, and reflection is a tool all men might better use to guide their daily thoughts. Upon opening a page at random today I read:

> *I believe that I . . . moved a man today. A wounded man in the field. Would that the exchange between us could be duplicated over all this bloody ground. An impossibility, I know, but nonetheless it gives me hope, even on this, the passing of my greatest defeat.*
>
> *I came to see my limits today.*
> *Then I saw myself surpass them. . .*

A cryptic message to the untrained eye, most surely. But what a flood of memories it produced: As my men and I made our retreat this fateful day, we were forced to ride back through the field of our failed endeavors, seeded now with the bodies of soldiers and watered with their blood. I was overcome with remorse at the thought of who would reap the dubious rewards such a crop would bring. My heart was in turmoil. Reading on, it remained thus:

> *Suddenly one of the enemy's fallen soldiers reached up with both arms from where he lay prostrate and bleeding. It seemed a gesture seeking succor, which surely I could not give him— but the medics would be along soon. Then he spoke, crying out with what could have been his last breath. He did not ask for God, or his loving mother. No sweetheart was bid good-bye. No, in a tone made of hatred and vengeance he hailed the victors of today's contest. He salted our wounds even as his own drained life from his limbs.*
>
> *I dismounted and approached the man. I could see on his face, through the black powder obscuring his features, that he was certain I was going to kill him. Were our roles reversed, perhaps he would gladly have slain me, and so expected to be treated in kind. I suppose I'll never know. Nor will I know what Providence led me to take that boy's hand and wish him a speedy recovery from his injuries.*
>
> *Through my tears, I saw the spitting hate of a nation embodied in a man today . . .*

Yet how well I recall seeing the soothing balm of moderation soften his broken heart.

Even in this bitter defeat I am blessed beyond all expectation. The so-called enemy and I saw eye-to-eye today and for one, precious moment there was no victor. No vanquished. Just men, coming to terms with their lots in life.

Moderation. An idea that is better stomached when one is older, I think. To be certain, some of my students swallow its demands as readily as a spoonful of castor oil. These are volatile times and it is so clear to me that the elixir of moderation would make life under the new regime so much more palatable.

Yet instead some young men seek the spice offered by grog shops, which I have begged the local regents to close. Still others are enticed by the unsavory fare offered by rabble rousing. Like spoiled children who did not get their way, these young hotheads think it neat to stand in the way of progress. They stamp their feet and thrash about in a tantrum of futility since the definition of progress has changed from what we had hoped.

Moderation in thought, word, and deed will carry us through these most difficult times, as it did when a victorious soldier met a defeated one and the two clasped hands in equanimity.

And so give heed to this: Disdain not the moderate soul for his lack of rashness, but instead embrace moderation in your own business dealings. For only through the clarity of vision that moderation inspires will you truly see each opportunity for its true value.

Tenacity

Reflecting upon the unfortunate occurrences of this past week, I am of the opinion that those dear men under my command may have lost the war, but they never lost their pride. And though the small force that they comprised eventually surrendered, they fought more bravely yet than did men twice their size and with reams more experience. Tenacity was their first name, duty their middle, and perseverance their last!

Many was a morning when the battlefield lay bloody with their friends and family members lying wounded or worse all around them, yet still these courageous men persevered on behalf of a cause they believed to be of preeminence. They had no uniforms, only the clothes on their backs. They had no supplies, only what they could find in the fields of battle or hunt in the wild. Their arms were old and outdated, their ammunition never sufficient to match that of their enemy.

They went without food when they hungered, without sleep when they tired, and without cure when they fell ill. They did without shoes in the winter and lumbered under backbreaking packs in the summer.

And they suffered not for one weekend, nor for one month. They carried on under great duress for years, always outnumbered, always outgunned. They hid behind trees and conjured like magicians to match wits with a much larger enemy who had every conceivable advantage over them.

In a war that divided a single country in half, this smaller force was left to fend for itself in an underdeveloped region with few technological advances. The larger side had all of the steel mills and factories, the cities and the manpower. They produced great weapons and uniforms, new cannons and guns. They trained and drilled and had manpower to pull from as casualties mounted, replacing each wounded or dead soldier with one who was younger, healthier, and better able to fight the enemy.

But what the smaller force lacked in resources, they made up for with tenacity and creativity. They looted each defeated battlefield for guns and ammunition, and even for supplies. Why, even their tents bore signs of their enemy's logos and factories, and they were not above ambushing their foe when they were greatly outnumbered.

It is said that fear makes men grow bold, but these men were motivated by honor and duty, courage and faith. They looked the enemy in the eye and met him toe to toe, and when they couldn't meet him toe to toe, they tripped him up or flushed him out.

Let this, too, be just the type of tenacity you need against your much bigger and better prepared opponents, whether upon the battlefield of business or in life. Meet them head on, and if they beat you down, meet them some other way. But meet them nonetheless. It is what your friends, your family, your compatriots, and your employees ask of you.

And it is all that you should ask of yourself...

Acceptance

This afternoon, two great opponents faced each other in a bitter contest that would test the wills of both their leaders. Much like boxers squaring off in the ring, these bloodied men were hard-pressed to return to their comers upon hearing the bell. Unlike boxers, however, there were other lives at stake beyond their furious fists.

One force was massive and powerful. Boasting unlimited funds, superior weaponry, expert training, and caches of fresh food, it trembled like a seething thing merely waiting to explode. Its soldiers were rested and fed, proud and strong, and despite numerous disappointments, were currently punishing their smaller, weaker foe with a barrage of lightning-quick assaults and thunderous violence.

The other side remained hungry yet fierce, weary yet defiant, and lacking any and all means to sustain themselves for much longer. They had been mighty warriors despite their small size and stature, bringing their worthy foe to its knees many times over the course of the campaign. But after years of numerous acts of bravery and heroism, this small force was finally wheezing its final, ferocious gasp.

As they woke to a chilly dawn that might see many men

dead by nightfall, the two sides anticipated yet another bloody day of brutality and vengeance. As the general of the smaller force, I rose early and sent out a lone rider to take stock of our situation. Not surprisingly, his report was unfavorable.

Our forces were outnumbered six to one, outgunned in front and behind, and a shipment of food that was supposed to arrive had been intercepted, leaving our tired troops dizzy from hunger and weak from exhaustion. Despite the troops' willingness to engage their enemy once more, I faced a life-altering decision: Push on at the risk of losing even more life and limb, with little hope of winning this battle, or face the inevitable. Like a condemned man at his own personal gallows, I considered my fate carefully and saw nothing but despair.

Despite the cause they'd been fighting for, despite the years of bravery I had personally witnessed from these beleaguered troops, despite the lives that had been lost and the blood that had been shed, it was time to pay the piper. A white flag was raised, a truce was called, and I met, albeit begrudgingly, with the general of the larger force, whose own mortality precluded him from celebration. Papers were hastily drawn, and a surrender was finally tendered.

In business as in life, no force can remain strong forever, no team can win every contest. Have faith enough to fight the good fight in all that you do, and strive to do your best on your own personal battlefield through the many seasons of your life. But if your best is simply not good enough, the only victory left to you is that of acceptance.

Accept the fact you have lost, and shake your opponent's hand graciously. You gain nothing by feeling bitter or angry, sad or confused. Instead, feel pride in a battle well fought, and accept your inevitable fate before moving on. In this way, you become ever stronger for tomorrow's battle, and the next day's, and the next. . . until success is the only inevitable outcome.

Courage

Like a ghostly wraith in the dead of night, fear is a constant companion to us mere mortals, whether in battle or in business, in life or in death. Every day, every night, every minute, every hour, there is always an insurmountable obstacle to fear. The challenge, then, is to counter those fears with a goodly amount of reasons not to be afraid.

On the battlefields of yesterday, good men trembled with fear quite frequently, and more easily than they would have you know. Fierce men, large men, bold men, and brave men, faced immeasurable odds and difficult tasks while their hands shook. While it is no sin to be afraid, to let that fear dominate the very thread of your existence robs you of your unlimited potential—and a vast amount of rest!

Today, for instance, I faced a formidable enemy across a battlefield not unlike the one we call "life." My men fought their enemy valiantly, but with only a fraction of the number or resources of their foe. These men were assaulted left and right, while all around them the enemy seemed to multiply with each fallen soldier.

I might have sounded the retreat, yet the field these men fought over proved to be a strategic military location to be defended at all costs, lest the enemy gain valuable ground and push my forces back even farther. Valiantly fought my men, while all around them friends and neighbors, and occasionally even family members, fell to the enemy's superior weaponry and fiery gaze.

Eventually, the men's resolve began to weaken. Too soon, brave soldiers who had fought with me in battle after battle holstered their weapons and ran past, their eyes averted, disappearing into the brush and fleeing the battlefield like so many mice from a sinking ship. Sensing a defeat I could not in good conscience afford, I pulled the sword from my scabbard and, sitting atop my fine and trusty steed, began a charge toward the enemy despite the fear that I, too, could lose my life as had so many of my men.

Closer and closer I drew, the hooves of my horse galloping on bloody soil as the men looked on in wonder and the beating of my heart shook the medals on my breast. Soon, they too took up the battle cry, and followed me into conflict. Even those who had fled returned to face their fate, and after too much bloodshed and not enough mercy, we turned our enemy away and were victorious.

But those of my men who would call me fearless would have been sorely mistaken. I was not a fearless man. Quite the contrary: I was full of fear. But I was also full of courage, which all men possess, and like all good men fought my fear to do what was right for myself, my men, and our forces at that moment.

Do not deny your fear in times of great distress or peril.

Instead, embrace this fear and use it to find the courage you must possess to face an enemy that may or may not be more formidable, dominant, and talented than you on the battlefield of life.

In this way you will be victorious, no matter what the ledgers of history record by your good name . . .

Obedience

"Obedience" is a term not often heard in the specific vocabulary of polite society, though many of my contemporaries are otherwise slaves to money and possessions, riches and fame. Do these harsh taskmasters not require obedience to their own unique sets of laws, rules, and codes? Do they not require a strict obedience that, if betrayed, brings forth personal disaster and financial ruin? Yet today saw my own obedience put to the test, though not for any reason so trivial as the aforementioned.

It has been known for some time that a great undercurrent of dissension runs through my country. From north to south, from east to west, a feeling of distrust and unease lies over hushed conversations and secret missives as thick as that of silt on the river bottom. While I myself am a military leader for my beloved country, I nonetheless feel a keen sense of duty for my homeland, in whose state the family manse resides.

As a country tears itself apart and states feel themselves pulled closer and closer to the unheard of act of secession, I myself feel as torn as the very nation itself. Are my fierce loyalties to lie with the country that so expertly trained me on the fields of battle, or with the people of my homeland, where my roots grow deep as the cottonwoods and my family resides to this day?

For an answer, I need only consult my very own heart. The place of my birth, long a comfort to my soul and respite for my weary bones, demands my fierce loyalty to its sacred soil. Though I have pledged allegiance to my country, my homeland owns my soul and it is thence where I must return to take up arms against those who would do it harm.

And so it is with a heavy heart that today I return home, leaving behind my countrymen and quarters, my old life for the new. Despite what history may record concerning those of us who turned our back on our country in favor of the land of our birth, the decision has been made and with obedience I head home, for better or worse.

Thus it is, with my honor intact, that my countrymen wave me goodbye and I to them. Though we may be enemies tomorrow, they are only doing the same as myself, pledging allegiance to the home of their birth, which they are duty-bound to defend, no matter what has been decreed on anything as fleeting as a mere piece of paper.

And so let it be with yourself. Though occupation and business may require much of your time, let not your heart deny the obedience to which it owes the rest of your livelihood. Mix business with pleasure, and balance your work life with family and friends at home. Let not yourself be consumed with matters of finance, but remain obedient to matters of the heart instead. For to grow rich in the soul is but a pathway to likewise filling your coffers!

Self Denial

It is with chagrin that I address today's unfortunate events, but address them I must if I am to fully understand the lessons they impart and their worth to my wounded conscience. For better or worse, my accomplishments have gained me a considerable amount of attention and notoriety. Like any nobleman in exile, I am neither hero nor villain, sinner nor saint.

Yet still my admirers come from all over the country. With trembling hands and modest hearts, they offer me gifts and souvenirs, services and opportunities that I am in no position to accept, let alone deserve. A humble man, I nonetheless have plenty of time to entertain such guests, albeit little patience for their offers. By reputation, I fear it is common knowledge that I have never suffered fools wisely, nor entertain those wolves who would visit in sheep's clothing.

Today, an eager young man came to me with a lucrative offer the likes of which few gentlemen ever receive, yet many would covet. Were I to understand his huckstering account of solid salesmanship correctly, I could earn ten times the amount of currency I was earning at my present employ if I would only accept this young man's generous offer.

And the offer? Simple. Too simple, in fact. All that was required of me was that I lend my famous, some would say "infamous," name to a certain institution, and I would be paid a handsome, not to mention "annual," fee. I would neither have to quit my current occupation, or move to my new place of employment. Simply by signing my name to a piece of paper and allowing this institution the use of that name in several pieces of promotional material per year, I could increase my income by tenfold and allow myself a sense of financial security unknown to honest men.

I am told that this type of behavior, though entirely immoral, is nonetheless entirely legal, and many of my counterparts were undertaking such consulting positions on a daily basis. My name would not be smeared nor would this transaction require any effort on my part whatsoever, short of signing the paper in front of me. That, and sleeping with myself each night, a task that would no doubt become more onerous as the implications of this offer were more fully exposed.

Naturally, I refused.

"Excuse me, sir," I informed my disappointed visitor. "I cannot consent to receive payment for services I did not render."

Despite the temptations surrounding you, work not for the easy dollar, but toil for your daily pay. After all, how else can you sleep at night, or ever hope to profit from your ill gains?

Self-denial. Concentrate not on the latter word, but the

former, and remain true to your self as you "deny" the offers of those that would tempt you with something for nothing, an equation well known to cause rising fortunes—and bankrupt souls.

Industry

Though I did not join the military to dig trenches, build bridges, or erect battlements, it is apparent that these very tasks should be my fate while I earn my stripes, and thus my pay. My current duty, more odious than most, is to build a protective fort upon a godforsaken island laid so prone to the elements that only four months work can be done upon it per year. And these occur quickly before the harsh fall and winter months deluge this spurned spit of land with storm upon storm, besmirching most, if not all, of the work done the very year before!

Were these the mild spring months, work might not be so distasteful. But as the land's native predator, the miniature but masterful mosquito, should be in residence those very same months, it is only during the brutal summer season in which this task can be undertaken. In heat that would drive a camel to shelter, toiling with supplies that leave much to be desired, it is my responsibility to forge as far ahead as possible to prepare for the harsh weather that will surely follow once our work is done.

On unsure ground and facing harsh conditions, my men and I toil round the clock to erect a battlement designed to weather the harsh test of time. Faithful they are, and true, but it is only so much any mere mortal can accomplish in one day, and even as the days pile up, the battle cry is lacking ferocity when it is known that half the day's work will be undone by erosion and decay practically overnight!

Yet toil we must, for the fort is strategic and its position essential to our country's safety, and so to rally each morning and rest each evening becomes the battle cry of our long, eventful days. Upon leaving our work at the end of the hot, industrious summer, it is with keen knowledge that we face facts: Half of what we have accomplished will be torn asunder by the fierce weather on the island during the harsh winter months. Bidding each other a fond adieu, we pledge to return on the morrow of next summer refreshed and renewed, invigorated and motivated.

And upon today's return to this embattled isle and its fractured fortress, we see that our instincts were correct: The hurricane gales of the winter months and the disarray of the spring have torn asunder much of our hard work and left only a fraction of the fort still standing. Harsh words are uttered, and worse, yet my men look to me for inspiration. Despite my weariness and fatigue upon just regarding the fort so recently torn asunder, the most I can do is sympathize. Yet all is not lost, and this time next year more will remain than once before. And a fraction more the year after, and again until our work here is finally done.

Thus it is that we return to our work, and it is only through our industry that this fort will one day be erected to ward off a foreign enemy from our hallowed soil. To work, men. Look not behind you, but in front, and stick to your task until it is won. Only in this way does anything ever get built, be it a building—or a man!

Encouragement

Many a contest of wills has been won—not by the acts of those men engaged in combat—but by the encouragement of their leader. By the time I was deemed worthy to take control over a large and powerful army of fierce and violent men, my military training had schooled me well in the fear these men were facing on their own personal battlefields each day.

Naturally, I felt responsible for these men, my men, and I did my best to encourage them as I saw fit. In the beginning I acted rashly, racing to lead my own men into battle like a fool with his first taste of power. Risking my own life, I assumed that only by example could I lead. Little did I know that I was leading myself into the path of destruction.

Through good fortune, and the love of my men, I managed to live through this period of reckless leadership. Eventually, this "fearless" leader realized that to court death with such relish and zest was not serving my men so much as myself. And though I was their general, be not mistaken, it was I that served them, as all great leaders must!

Instead, I learned to encourage them with words of praise or calming effect, and never allowed myself to entertain harsh and bitter diatribes against their cowardice or weakness. Each dawn I had to muster my men into battle. And many a conflict saw less of those men return. New men joined my ranks, and veterans were lost, and so, surrounded by strangers, I forged new bonds in a process not unlike a drill sergeant preparing young boys to be men.

But to win the cause, battles had to be waged. More importantly, these contests had to be won. I knew that these were good, strong, and brave men, yet they often had to be reminded of that very fact themselves! No longer could I court disaster by rashly leading my men into battle. Instead, I was charged with the task of making them see, through my words and my deeds off of the battlefield, that what they were doing was right and just, even at a cost so high and precious as a human life.

In the end, my men grew to love me much as I loved them. Through daily encouragement, I allowed them to be the men they always knew they could become, and in doing so learned the unique difference between true leadership—and true vanity.

Like a general, you must find the words to lead your team to victory, and cheer them on from the sidelines as they either win or lose. Your words are just as important as their actions, and without you they would be alone on the battlefield, like a soldier without his general...

Leadership

I think it better to do right, even if we suffer in so doing, than to incur the reproach of our conscience—and posterity. This thought I tried in all things to impart to my men, and then to the boys under my care in the college. If one is capable of leading, then it becomes one's most excellent duty to do so.

I have led both men and boys to their deaths in war. I have led them to victory as well, but the pain of one does long outlast the exaltation of the other. This is doubly so, since our victories came only in the contests, but escaped us in the war. We had, I was satisfied, sacred principles to maintain and rights to defend for which we were in duty bound to do our best, even if we perished in the endeavor—but in the end it fell to me to dash the hopes of nation.

Yet still I lead, though the weight of a defeated people bears heavy upon my shoulders. I accept the burden with full responsibility. Such is the price of leadership.

If the leader is discharging his duty to the best of his ability, then it will not be surprising that he should inspire in other men a sense of admiration, an attitude of respect. The evocation of these feelings can pull from men acts of heroic proportion, but the leader should beware of undue adulation. Hero worship is unseemly, and can oft lead to defeat. Expecting the impossible of one's men does not mean they can achieve the impossible, and rest assured they will feel their failures more keenly than you. I know it because I read it in the eyes of those who survived one of our greatest defeats. Their pain lay not in the failure itself, but in the perception that they had failed their leader.

And still I lead, always remembering that I am not infallible, nor the men below me. Such is the pitfall of leadership.

The best thing a leader can do is to create other leaders, to imbue the spirit of those under his care or command with the confidence to think for themselves, and the skill to deal with those who cannot lead. My greatest lieutenant, proposing an unorthodox plan of attack that would leave me with troops numbering only one third of the army opposing us, had no fear in making so daring a proposal. Such was my faith in this man, and in the color of our time together, that I authorized him with hardly more than a shake of my head. As a result, one of our greatest victories ensued.

So still I lead, ever grateful for competent men. Such is the reward of leadership—a reward to be reaped by yourself, in abundance, should you only follow my lead.

Reflection

I have lately returned from a ride in the county, cut short a little by sudden rain. So in lieu of physical exercise I will put these few minutes to good use and exercise my mind.

Were it not for my daily sojourns into solitude, whether on my horse or my own two feet, I believe I would never have lived this long, nor become a man who has led armies, raised children, guided a nation, and built a university. These accomplishments, which some hail as greatness, though I see them only as avenues of my duty as a man of honor, are all due in large part to half an hour a day spent alone in the woods, thinking of things other than they.

Other habits, certainly, contribute to my health at this late date, among them a firm bedtime of 10 o'clock. I have long believed that one hour of sleep before midnight is worth two after that magic time. A man exhausted simply cannot fully apply his faculties to the given problems of a day. Generals who work well into the night are doing a disservice to their troops, despite appearances of their diligence. Soldiers need a leader who is alert and prepared, not harried by fatigue.

Time spent with my two best-loved books has served me

well also. One author wrote, hundreds of years before I was born: "Misfortune nobly borne is good fortune." That statement rings so true for me, and has been a beacon of hope throughout my life, that it surely feels emblazoned upon my very soul. Today, on this rainy afternoon, I can look back at my endeavors with an easy mind. From great to small, success to failure, I know that even when things went awry, they did so in the midst of the absolute best intentions and efforts. Some good always comes out of everything, even if one cannot see it at the time.

The loss of a war led to the rebirth of a nation. Fire in the forest is necessary if the young trees are to grow.

These things I have time to dwell upon—and so make my peace—because I make the time. My days, once filled with soldiers and smoke, are today brimming only with appointments and administration. I could easily remain shackled to my desk, but this half hour of time with myself is crucial, not just to my own well-being, but to the quality of my work and the proper execution of my duty.

Action must by garnished by reflection, lest it be reduced to ineffectual flailing, which results just as surely in the drowning man's death as never learning to swim. Take heed, as well, to make the time for daily reflection, lest you suffer the moral weakness of an unexamined soul.

Family

My young son once taught me a lesson—unknowingly—that has stayed with me through all my campaigns, both during and after the war. He and I had decided to go for a walk one winter afternoon. As we walked I fell into my usual reflection and my much longer strides put me rather ahead of him. Realizing that he was no longer at my side, I turned back to offer my assistance. What I saw left its mark on me.

There was my boy, diligently making his way across the deeply snowed ground. His shoulders were square, his chin held high, and he was conscientiously trying to set his little feet, one after the other, in the center of my boot prints. I realized then that it behooved me to walk very straight, if this little fellow was already following behind me—literally in my footsteps.

Only family can touch one so deep, and have an effect that lasts into the grave. Family and faith have shaped the man who writes here today. All else has followed after.

I write while my daughter sleeps nearby, fitfully. She has fallen ill and I feel her fever as if it burned in my own skin. Nothing pleases me more than to wipe the sweat from her brow, to hold her pallid hand. Nothing, that is, but that I could soon see her well.

I have not left her side for days, nor bear I any desire to do so. I sleep on a cot in her room, my ears bent to the slightest change in her breathing. It is a role I know well. My mother was invalid during my youth and, having an absent father, it fell to me to be her caretaker. I am thankful now, that experience having prepared me somewhat for this—and many others much like it. But what parent can prepare for his child's pain? My throat constricts, my heart stops, each time she coughs; when she sleeps I fear she will not awake.

A parent's love is fierce in all its forms.

Of course, happier days dapple my memory like a sun on a meadow. After the war I treasured those precious days when my family surrounded me. My wife, sons, daughters, their friends. A house full of laughing young people is a home truly blessed.

Even those times when a child is in need of guidance—those times are a gift as well, for what parent does not wish to share the wealth of his knowledge with the younger generation? Always their best interest motivates our hearts. We endeavor to shield them from false expectations and disappointments. We strive to keep them grounded, and to appreciate the sparse gifts that truly have meaning in this world, instead of chasing the wind. We impart breeding and character. We guide them toward proper adulthood, as young gentlemen and ladies.

A man too busy to immerse himself in the joys of family is a hollow man indeed. No conquering general, no business tycoon, ever had greater wealth than that which can be found in the sheltering arms of his family.

Fame and fortune are meager comforts when the gales of old age blow through to the bones. And while a sound business plan is worth its weight in gold—a family investment is indeed without price.

Order

Today I made a silent statement. As my students and I marched in procession with our neighboring college, I deliberately marched out of step, ignoring the beating drum and stomping feet around me. A small act, really, but one representative of my desire to change the system, however difficult that might be. Walking out of step with my compatriots, ignoring the driving rhythm of the drum, that took all my concentration, all my willpower.

While my heart is glad for the example I set, I still cannot help pondering the paradox that faces me as a shaper of young men. How does one maintain order while encouraging free thought?

Order. It has many faces, and those faces populate the crowd of values I hold dear. They are a welcome sight in the chaos of modern life, like a cup of tea by the fireside on a blustery night. But order for order's sake alone is simply a mask for weakness of mind and spirit. It is for he who follows without thinking, as well as he who leads without thought.

It has fallen to me, it seems, to spend my days in the service of educating young men. Although my heart longs for the sweetness of an agrarian life, where order and nature wear the same face, the seasons following one another without complaint, I find I shall not be allowed that rest. Instead my days are filled with the volatile thoughts and actions of young men, which I must govern as best I can through my own example.

Yet again I assert, let there be no needless rules. Let discipline come from the heart of honor and self-respect that lies within each of my students. I will not force them to adhere to some arbitrary code of conduct. They carry inside themselves all the tools necessary for appropriate behavior. It is my duty to draw out from these boys what they may not know is there and teach them to live their lives by it.

But herein lies my quandary: How does one set the example for civility, honor, duty, and loyalty while seeking to change the system governing those very beliefs? Here at this institution I see the desperate need for change, but how can I achieve that while maintaining the attitudes of respect and obedience that I demand of my young men? Can I fly in the face of tradition without encouraging my students to act as capriciously as myself?

Are working for change and inciting rebellion only varying shades of gray?

And so it is thus: Order must be maintained, but the system must change. The two must blend together else I misled these boys in their search for character.

I can only hope that today's statement reaches the intended ears. I did it because it must be done, just as making changes at the college over which I preside must happen for the betterment of my students. And for the betterment of my country, so lately ravaged by war.

I will do whatever it takes. But at all costs, I will maintain order. I will follow proper channels and continue to set the tone for the youth who look to me for such. And through those channels I will succeed. On many fronts.

As for yourself, fear not the chain of command that stretches throughout your organization. Instead, use it to modify your company's weaknesses, encourage its strengths, and maintain its overall order. Thus will you effect true change—by true order.

Humor

The high commander of the opposition saw fit to replace one of his generals today. Oh how I shall miss him. Such a connection we had: We understood each other so well that I felt I could anticipate his every move...

Perhaps now is not the time for humor, but I find in brevity such succor for my soul. Laughter reminds me—and those around me—that I am simply a man, no more, no less. Subtle wit is exercise for my mind and relief to my spirit.

I read once that the great generals of Caesar's time would parade around their cities, displaying their captives and spoils. These men employed a slave to trail along behind them, reminding them that fame is fleeting and that they are mere mortals. Better they had shared a good jest!

The man who is too serious builds a wall around his heart, shutting others out while sealing himself in. That is a living death I could not bear. Lightness of spirit brings relief to the most difficult of situations, and added joy to the happiest. Laughter is indeed the best medicine, and the most gentle physician.

It is unfortunate, then, that humor can as easily be a sour draft when doled out with the wrong intent. Laughter at the expense of another—the intentional disparagement of a person's character for the sake of a paltry snicker from someone so unworthy as to respond to cruelty—this is misuse. The true gentleman curbs a sharp tongue unless he is sure of the object's stalwart self-image, and is likewise willing to turn that same satirical bent upon himself.

But when I think of the blessings attendant upon a good sense of humor, one that lifts others up, I cannot help but remember a gift I once received. A kind lady had crocheted for my family a teapot warmer and an afghan. To my children's delight I popped the warmer on my head and then draped the afghan round my shoulders, all the while dancing a jig. It's a sight I'm sure none of them will forget—especially since they delight in reminding me of it whenever we have company!

Ever have I been an advocate of decorum, of good deportment. These things I consider imperative, without a doubt. And yet the ability to diffuse a situation, to avoid unpleasantness in social settings through a well-placed word or well-timed act: that is a skill any gentleman worth his salt would cultivate.

For though business may grow dim and tense, never fail to miss an opportunity to lighten the atmosphere at work. Be it a well-timed grin or a self-effacing riddle, let the good doctor of humor make many calls to your place of business, for the healthiest—and happiest—company is often the most successful.

Tolerance

Though it is not the first time I have felt thus, let me be the first to admit it: I am at a loss. Continually I remind the denizens of my beloved land that they must move forward, that they must turn eyes filled with tolerance toward those they once called enemy. If not, no true healing can begin. If not, we all are lost.

A battle was waged here. Hearts were hardened in the fiery forge of war. Many brave men were taken before their rightful time. These things I, of all people, know too well. But unless we begin the process of reconciliation, those men who died in the past will have died in vain because the men of the future will have no hope of overcoming. Until we can learn to tolerate our brethren from across a border that is no more, we will remain in this state of abasement.

If our hearts remain hard we can blame no one but ourselves when things do not change. Why, simply consider today's recent event: A woman whose family lands were damaged during the fighting called upon me to help her seek amends. Specifically, an ancestral tree was destroyed. It had shaded her family with kindness for generations and she felt keenly its loss.

I looked upon the tree for some minutes, remembering all the devastation I'd seen, thinking of the ruin of my own family lands, where enemy soldiers had been laid to rest as a personal attack upon me. I knew that she expected my sympathies, wanted me to commiserate with her upon the terrible evils that had been inflicted upon us by a ruthless enemy.

But conciliation was the tune I sang for her. It is imperative that we as a country move on, just as this woman must indeed move on and begin repairing her life and property. We can do nothing else, and tolerance is the key to our progression.

When I think of the need for tolerance I think back on the first vacation I took after leaving my position in the military. A miniature war was being waged at the country resort where I and my family took our rest and I was called upon yet again by my honor to serve as leader and tactician.

Certain parties were visiting this lovely retreat who were deemed by the bulk of the guests to be "from the other side." Alas, the war had been over for years, but many people still thought in terms of "us" and "them." I took it upon myself to make welcome these folks, because I knew that in my person I represented all the attitudes and the behaviors of what my people could be, especially the newest crop of youthful socialites.

I made it a point of honor to engage these shunned souls in conversation, to take tours of the grounds with them, to be solicitous in all things. My actions went a long way toward salving the wounds as yet unhealed, as I knew they would. For it so often falls to me to set the example of tolerance that will bring both side of this conflict together again. I undertake this task with relish.

And so should you. Though it is rarely easy to be tolerant of those souls less compassionate—or qualified—than you, seek not to rail against them, but instead entreat them learn from your example. For by example must you lead, all the while following the rocky trail of tolerance.

Responsibility

I did not want to return to that sacked city, laid so low when I could not hold it any longer. Even my own son's wedding was nearly not enough to draw me back. Those people had been my responsibility and my best was not enough to stave the flood of enemy troops that surged over them, over their homes. Over their hearts.

The thought of going back was a newly honed knife playing at the puckered flesh of an old scar—one I vainly thought had lately healed.

Only my son's earnest pleas, made in person after a long journey of hard riding, could have persuaded me. With a deep breath I made my decision. I thought, "My presence is required then, it seems. To honor my family I must face the consequences of my defeat, walk the field so fraught with memories of my failure. If it must be, then I will go forward with a stout heart. Let the knowledge that I did my best clear my conscience. Let it be the banner waving above me in the stiff wind of absolution."

And so I undertook to attend my son's marriage to a lovely girl in a city that bore difficult associations for me. Sadly, the trip coincided with a far less pleasant gathering that also required my attendance: I was due in court. I had been summoned to defend my military actions in the recent conflict, the one that had left my beloved cause and country afflicted with poverty and devastation.

The court, as it turns out, tried in vain to retire my sense of responsibility, their goal being to condemn another man with accountability for my actions. They implied that I had not acted of my own volition, but had been merely a pawn for those in power above me.

This notion offends me to the very marrow of my bones. If it were true, would I dread so the return to a place where I had fought and lost?

Only a shameless and craven man would allow another to stand in his stead when there is a price to be paid. I did what I did, for good or ill, using all the manifold skills and experiences at my disposal to make the best decisions in difficult circumstances.

Men died and a city burned—countless men and many cities—as a direct result of my actions. These things I accept, though my failure is bitter gall. Let no one take this responsibility from me: If my best should yield rewards, then I will readily share those rewards with my compatriots. But if it should yield failure, then I will just as readily acknowledge my hand in those dealings as well. I will accept the consequences bravely, and endeavor to make a new start from the ashes I have created with the flame of my actions.

Would you not do the same? Though the heat of responsibility may flicker at your toes, stand fast to suffer the consequences of your own actions. Fear not, however. For the actions of an honorable man bow low the highest flames, causing him to walk unharmed to the altar of success.

Example

Finally, I am returned to the field for whose honor I fought so hard. The victor of many contests, I still have left this particular war in defeat. But for the love of my family, and the steady knowledge that I did my duty in the face of insufferable odds, I should be left bereft.

Devastation surrounds me, the markings of struggle catching my eye at every turn. Yet I have not truly lost if I can turn people's eyes away from the precipice of defeat and lift their careworn faces into the bright sun of a new day. That day can dawn only with their commitment, their investment in good things to come in a far off future. It falls to me to show them the way.

I want only to retire into the loving arms of my family, to secure for myself and for them a quiet place in the country, away from the demands of my position, but I know that it is my example—and perhaps my example alone—that can raise spirits weighed down by the yoke of despair. Under my command hands made idle by anger and bitter resentment must be filled with the weapons of recovery: pride, self-sacrifice, and the belief that good, honest work can truly make a difference.

They watch me keenly now. I am the embodiment of this

place, and I share their lot. Every word I form, every action I take, sets the tone for their recovery—or their demise. As it was from the beginning, it is even more so now: I can make their days here bearable by treating them with respect, by listening to their ideas and problems. Or I can close my door to them, let them make their own way without guidance, and then blame them later when things are not as I planned. The choice, invariably, is mine.

I am responsible for the tenor of activity in this place.

If I shirk my duties, why should they not? If I play false and gloss over trouble, why should they not? Who can expect them to be more than their leader? I can only expect them to do what is right, and what is right in this setting is determined by myself.

If I demand the best of myself, they will not balk when I demand the best of them. In fact, they will find pride in being able to give me their best. Some may not know what their best is, but they will define it by looking to me. They will take pleasure in quality. They will find satisfaction in discovering reserves of strength they thought depleted. They will rejoice in doing what may have seemed tedious before.

All this rests on my shoulders. I must carry myself appropriately, both in this defeat and in the victories yet to come. In these and all things my example is the only weapon I have against mediocrity, sullen rancor and inactivity.

So, too, find yourself: Preach not to those in your employ, lest they grow weary of your sermons. Yet lead by example instead, that they may be inspired by your actions—and mimic them in their own.

Compassion

Was it not enough for me to lose a contest so hard fought and bloody, to injure my pride and my livelihood to return to a land once besieged, now thoroughly defeated? Yet upon my arrival, to find that enemy forces had occupied my own family home, and refused to allow me passage through its hallowed doors.

If only to say goodbye . . .

Naturally, it was known to me that throughout the conflict my family farm was in danger of being occupied by our crafty foe. Through dispatches and urgent missives, the news was first hinted at, then rumored, and finally proved to be an unfortunate fact. Though my heart was heavy, my family was safe, and that was all that was of immediate import to me.

Upon returning to my homeland, however, it galled me to see occupying forces lounging where my family once had, enjoying the splendor of a manse once so familiar and warm to those of my kinship, now squandered for the satisfaction of a harsh and brutal enemy. I knew, of course, that there were legal avenues I could have pursued to regain the rightful ownership of my family's land.

Many in my defeated army, and indeed my own family, from whom the prodigal manse had been taken, urged me to do so. "That land is yours," they cautioned. "Regain what you so rightfully deserve." But it was among these violent ministrations that I learned that my once valuable farmland was being used for a much grimmer prospect: The enemy's doomed and fallen soldiers had been buried in once fertile soil, their empty husks all that remained of their former fighting selves. Souls had been reaped, and now grew high to the heavens from fields in which my children had once played.

Furthermore, it was learned that plans were being made to honor these buried dead by turning the old homestead into a national cemetery. A hallowed institution in which their bereaved families could at last pay tribute to their fallen sons, brothers, nephews, and uncles. Would regaining ownership of my land displace these wounded souls, who had fought so valiantly against my own brave warriors? Would the families left behind not shudder and moan upon hearing that I had regained my land, only to displace their dead?

There was no way I could consider this option, and thus I never pursued regaining this property after the war. Instead, I moved into a rented house and now live here peaceably in the knowledge that many grieving families will profit from my compassion, while only my own would have profited from my greed.

And what could you learn from this story? Perhaps you

will win on the battlefield of life, and your opponent will lose. They may be bitter, and hurtful, and feel betrayed. And you will feel exultant, triumphant, and elated. But have compassion upon your enemy, and above all be a graceful winner. Shake their hands, and offer them condolences, and look forward to meeting them again in the future.

In that case, you will have won twice!

Overconfidence

Much as a general performs, a good leader influences through his actions, his words, his thoughts, and his deeds. He instructs, he encourages, he brings to bear every single year of his experience on each and every situation, minor or major, vital or insignificant. At times, a general can be all things to his troops: mother, father, friend, stern taskmaster, or a gentle listener. An overconfident general, however, can be his troops' worst enemy! Like a spy among the faithful, this vain man constitutes a threat unseen among the troops, and like a virus draws many with him to their death.

In recent months I had amassed great victories, and the notches on my belt were too numerous to record. I strode with confidence, some would say too much confidence, from battlefield to battlefield, presiding in victory over yet another contest fought hard and won valiantly by my brave troops. Though it was always myself who claimed the victory.

As with all things, however, my overconfidence proved to be as dangerous as my enemy. For after a string of victories that had many believing the war would soon be won, today I rushed into one too many a battle without my legendary caution or consideration. Forgetting that human life was at stake, if only momentarily, I made a rash decision and forged ahead when caution would have proved the better part of valor.

As a result, I suffered a staggering defeat that will no doubt be recorded in history as one of the worst in recent memory. Many lives were lost, too many to mention aloud without descending into deep despair, and even more were injured, through my own personal vanity. Who was I to lead these men to their fate so hastily? Who was I to think that no one could conquer me? Who was I to feel heady at all of those victories stacked behind me like so many cemetery crosses?

After all, in the face of such a monumental and costly defeat, who even remembered any of those victories at all?

And so, in battle as in life, be wary of overconfidence in yourself. Be vigilant against this emotion in your everyday dealings, and be careful when you find yourself growing too eager or too bold to conquer an unknown foe, simply because you can. Time is a harsh taskmaster, and rushing into one too many a business deal or merger can mean months, if not years, of hard work tossed to the wind.

Confidence is an honorable, and in today's world a necessary, trait.

Overconfidence, however, is a sin of vanity, and one not easily forgiven by the ravages of time or commerce. When people look at you, is that the smile of confidence they see?

Or the shifty smirk of overconfidence?

Discipline

It is known that a great leader is occasionally born, but most are just as surely made. No leader can possibly lead if someone else has never led him, and no ruler can rule without first being ruled himself. Thus it was that I was fortunate enough to attend a great school for military cadets in my impressionable youth. Lush and wooded, it had been home to some of the greatest military leaders any country has ever produced.

But none attained such status by doing whatever they wanted, whenever it suited them. These great leaders were forged, not by fire, but instead by discipline so firm it would break the weak, and exhaust the merely mediocre. Above all else, military life breeds a fierce allegiance to discipline. A force of trained soldiers would be nothing without the rules they'd learned to follow in their strict training—and no battle could be won by a force intent on anarchy.

Where to go, what to do, how to do it: Such seemingly insignificant matters are all governed by the rules that were so ingrained in them, and myself, back at the academy. As a matter of fact, rules were so important at this military academy that if even the smallest one was broken, a demerit was given to the cadet who had made the transgression.

Shoes not polished right? Give that cadet one demerit. Late for roll call? Give that cadet five demerits. Your uniform not cleaned and pressed? That's seven demerits for you, cadet! Day in and day out, every facet of each minute, each hour, was governed by rules. How to hold your fork. How fast you had to eat. Where you could eat. When you could talk. When you couldn't talk. How loud you could talk.

Always, in the back of the cadet's mind, as it was in mine, was how to follow these rules and avoid receiving a single demerit, for this was the equivalent not only of dishonor to the cadet's school, but also to his country. Above all, duty was important to a cadet. And in this man's army, rules were his duty!

Upon this very day, at the conclusion of four arduous years of honor and duty, each cadet was informed of his demerit totals. Four years of following rules, obeying commands, and avoiding demerits. 22 demerits for this cadet, 63 for that one. 15 over here and 36 over there. When I was finally to receive my totals, I reported eagerly to learn how I had done. What was my total of demerits? Not a one. In four long years, I had never earned a single demerit. Day after day, week after week, and year after year, I followed the rules and followed them well.

In all that time, I never held my fork wrong. Or polished my shoes less than perfectly. Or spoke out of turn. Or showed up late for my drills. Or ate too slow or slept too late or walked too fast or looked left when I was supposed to look right.

But then, why would I? Fortunate enough to attend a school that trained a nation's presidents and generals, its esteemed senators and congressmen, how then could I avoid the very discipline that had forged such leaders as these? It was my duty, and my honor, to obey every rule I encountered.

Without rules, I fear, society would crumble, and men would be unprepared for the destiny that awaits us all. Shirk not your duty, and adhere to discipline, for these are the pillars on which your very conscience rests!

Delegation

To be a successful leader, as opposed to merely an adequate one, one must do more than rant and rave, instruct and defend. One must observe a situation, remedy the ills, and delegate authority to staff and officers alike. For a powerful leader, this is often a most onerous undertaking, and one not relished by many in such positions of authority.

Today, however, I felt the need to delegate my authority in a way I never had before, and was rewarded with a victory unlike any other. One the eve of a great battle, one of my best officers came to me for counsel. In the end, I fear our roles were reversed. For as a unique plan unrolled from his eloquent lips, I was shocked at his mastery of military strategy, and found myself seeking his counsel on such matters in turn!

After all, it is quite common for an old war-horse such as myself to become stuck in his ways, falling back time and again on the tired path of least resistance, like the ruts in a road over which a wagon passes again and again. If it has brought us victory before, let us not waver from it for fear of defeat. This new strategy, however, gave me much to consider, and even more to fear. It bordered on the insane to begin with, and in its telling my enthusiastic comrade became quite overzealous himself. I feared for his sanity, though all the while his words made perfect sense.

Considering the situation, I had only two choices: I could refuse this passionate man's request to try the impossible, or I could succumb to his will and delegate my authority to allow him to try as he may with a plan that could have been either rash or brilliant. (Though secretly, it appeared to be both at the very same time!)

Yet he was a sane man and a true leader, rallying his troops yet and again to victories few thought possible under the circumstances, and never giving me pause to consider his tactics, which were nothing short of brilliant.

Was I to win this war by myself? Was I to oversee every scrap of food in my soldier's gullet or lump of lead in their barrels? What single man could be privy to every piece of intelligence, every lesson of strategy, every change in the tide of battle? What man, no matter how wise or sage, could win each battle on his own?

Thus it was that I regarded this officer carefully and uttered three words, and three words only: "Go to it."

Without pause, he left my tent and did just that. Hours later, he returned victorious, and affirmed my suspicions that he was indeed as brilliant as I'd hoped. Acting rashly without counsel is ludicrous, but so is attempting to fight every battle by one's self. No man can do it all, and by surrounding oneself with the best advisors and staff, he is able to have many heads, many ears, many arms and many hearts.

Delegate authority to those you trust, and trust only those whom your heart smiles upon. In this way will your efforts succeed, not in spite of delegating your authority, but because of doing so!

Diplomacy

One who was once my enemy, whose leadership I have now embraced fully in both word and deed, called upon me for a visit today. Diplomacy demands that I had little choice and must attend upon his wishes. When last we met it was to put an end to senseless killing. It was an end for which many of my men would rather have continued to die.

I did not want to make the trip this time, as before. Too many memories awaited me, their main purpose to turn my boots from forward progression into the morass of regret and self-doubt. Difficult decisions again had to be made prior to meeting with this great general-turned-statesman.

I did not wear the gray.

These other clothes seemed somehow mean, undignified and beneath the man I was about to join. But I knew that my usual habit had in the past inspired feelings of unrest. I did not want to pull at the fragile sutures knitting together the rift in this only newly united nation. Like so many in my recent past, it was a difficult decision. Was I betraying my people? Was I playing the chameleon, who changes shades to suit his surroundings and therefore is never to be trusted?

As I have from the beginning, I wanted to avoid conflict

by sowing the seeds of renewal; reconciliation was my muse. I wanted a clean slate, one on which a new history could be written by a people who would never forget the old one, poised for a moment on the edge of glory.

Giving up the gray was hardly more vexatious than was my first act of what many saw as capitulation: taking the oath to uphold the laws and principles of the new administration. Scores upon scores of my most zealous supporters believed I had betrayed them. This belief was anathema to me, but duty required that I do whatever was in my power to restore stature to my people. I consciously made the decision to set an example that would go far toward smoothing furrowed brows on both sides.

As it turns out, my action spurred thousands to take the oath as well, although it was bitter to them, for a time heightening barely faded feelings of rancor. Yet what advance does not come served with fear as a side dish?

Therefore heed well the comfort provided by tact. In meetings both large and small, take care to act the diplomat, and not the fool. Diplomacy, though sometimes costly in its immediacy, is well worth the price of future harmony.

Temptation

In times of crises or conflict, great men often rise to power, fame, and glory. And so it was with myself, for after leading my troops into battle I was rewarded with a life of prestige and honor. Though some considered me a handsome man in my youth, it is said that I grew only more so as I aged. (Though my own mirror often disputed this very fact!)

My stature improved with my legend, and my hair and beard grew white with dignity and only added to my apparently regal appearance. I dressed formally, not to mention well, and my daily exercise kept my figure firm and masculine.

Consequently, many of my most ardent admirers were women, and despite the fact that I was married, and happily so, these ladies pursued me endlessly, from party to party, engagement to engagement, even stopping me on the street to talk, laugh, and flirt.

For my sake, I must admit that this man of minor stature and undeserved fame thoroughly enjoyed the company of young and attractive females, for which I fortunately never lacked. My laughter rang through the dance halls and parties that I was forced to attend due to my rank and station, and I played the part of the humble host or set upon gentleman as if at center stage.

Still, I am a man of honor who remains faithful to my wife, throughout the early years when I was an unknown military cadet, as well as the years that saw my stature rise with each passing day. Despite the attention of attractive and willing females, I am a gentleman and never succumbed to indiscretions, nor indeed ever considered it except in passing or fleeting moments of weakness or shame.

In letters to young women who would write, or to friends on the matter of such young women, I never speak in any tone other than playful or innocent, always reminding my female pursuers that I am a married man and entirely unavailable to them, no matter how flattering their attention might be to an old man such as myself.

And I am. Had I been a confirmed bachelor, my life might have been very different. Yet I've married and exchanged vows, and through the good times and the bad, I remain faithful despite temptation nearly every year for the twilight of my life.

Consider temptation, and deny it each time. For only by sacrificing illicit temptations can you truly enjoy the contentment of a life lived well—and a heart most pure.

Humility

As I was pulling on my boots before mass this morning, that seemingly insignificant chore nonetheless reminded me of how often it has become man's folly to think too much of himself, especially in the face of great accomplishments or financial wealth.

After all, it was my destiny to become a leader of men, for better or worse. For years my so-called bravery and ingenuity, my supposed strength and courage were legendary, and these served me well in my public life after the war. As years passed and my reputation grew, however, it has lately become hard for me to go anywhere without a crowd assembling to cheer me on or offer me their well wishes for a life well led, and a heart most pure.

Whether it be the marketplace or the stable, the side of the street or even my front stoop before the morning news, I am accosted on all sides by fervent fans and overzealous crowds. There are sketches made of me for the newspapers, and fine portraits done of me for the sake of history, and even photographs made to preserve my likeness for the history books, which will no doubt record of me equal parts good fortune and folly.

Men travel hundreds of miles, if only to shake my hand or raise their hats, while women fawn, and often fight, over me, all in plain view of my wife! There are parades and applause, tributes and editorials, all praising my supposed past triumphs and very real tragedies, or my mainly undeserved reputation for valor and bravery.

So how can I ever retain my sanity amid all of this petty pomp and crass circumstance? How can I keep my ego in check when everyone surrounding me sings my praises like songbirds greeting the new day? How can I keep my humility in the face of such worship from my ardent admirers and fervent fans?

Fortunately, I have a family that grounds me, and reminds me daily, with glee, might I add, that in between the daguerreotypes and the pressing of the flesh, there are chores to tend to and fences to mend. As many a great man has discovered, the swell of applause and warm embrace of admirers is little match for an overflowing ash can or swollen gutters!

I also keep my life simple with routine and tradition, taking my breakfast early in the morning before attending mass and then riding my favorite horse for exercise each afternoon—visitors, photographers, biographers or no.

But this "great" man has a little secret: My feet are exceptionally small, almost childlike, a fact that few of my admiring public knows about, but that I can't help but notice each morning when I rise! After all, I have to slip first one tiny foot and then the other into nearly childlike socks, and then put on almost infantile shoes every morning of my life. After all, whose head could get too big when his feet are so very small?

In between trumpeting your own horn and rushing to bring forth your many strengths, you would do well to recall your weaknesses, be they mental or physical, to keep you humble in those times when you are feeling the least bit boastful!

Chivalry

Alas, a great nation was torn in two by a fierce contest that raged on for years and cost the lives of many countrymen. Naturally, only one side of this conflict could emerge victorious, and when it did, I returned home to my native land defeated, arriving there to face the people in whose honor I had tried to fight so valiantly.

Despite their grief, these humble people never turned on me, and I was truly grateful for their unwavering loyalty. Unfortunately, the same could not be said for those who were victorious over us. As the celebrations faded away and the country tried to heal its wounds, the victors of this war quickly turned on the defeated. Like a tiger who's been grabbed by the tail, they lashed out with teeth ready to tear flesh and open old wounds so recently starting to heal.

As the defeated force's leader, naturally I was left alone to face the brunt of this anger. I was accused of treason, brought before several courthouses devoid of any justice whatsoever, and my name was disparaged in newspapers and grog shops throughout the land. My reputation was sullied, my very life threatened, and those who would proudly call themselves victors cast dispersions on my character at every opportunity, no matter how minor or grand.

Yet somehow I never lost sight of the fact that where once the nation had been torn in two, it was now trying to heal itself again. As the victor wrought its vengeance upon the land and property of the defeated, those they persecuted threatened to retaliate with more violent opposition and words of anger. Like scorpions on the desert sand, the two sides clashed again as promises were broken and rumors spread, but all the while I spoke of peace, forgiveness, and of the healing process that must accompany all tragedies. Not unlike that of the grief that follows a death, this process of healing must take place before we could ever call ourselves countrymen again.

Never loud or bitter, never vengeful or angered, I tried to calm the crowds that sought my counsel, and attempted to speak with wisdom and foresight about the future. What was best for the country at this delicate crossroads was that they put aside their differences and take up the healing process we all so desperately needed. Instead of urging my countrymen to take up arms yet again, I stressed the importance of forgiveness, of turning the other cheek, and of working for peace and prosperity in a war-torn country that was sorely in need of both.

Many historians have spoken of my gentle words and more importantly, my chivalry, as contributing to the peace efforts that saved the country yet another bloody battle, even after the war had been won. While I hadn't managed to lead my forces to victory, in defeat I had set my sights on something more important: peace for my people.

To do the same, whether it be in business or in life, remember that a code of honor exists between men, and to hold fast to that chivalrous code during both fortune and misfortune. How easy it would have been for me to retaliate against those enemy forces that would have done me harm, and how tempted I was at times to do just that. But the code of chivalry denies such petty satisfactions, and history has proven my actions to be the cause of great comfort to many people.

Let your personal history read as mine did: Be kind and gentle, wise and true, and let not the frenzy of your time dictate the will of your own, chivalrous heart!

Faith

If ever I feel far from my God, I simply mark a path to the woods—or the mountains or the fields. Each of these in its own way displays the glory that is God and inspires me in both thought and deed. On a solitary ride my head becomes clear and my troubles resolve themselves into challenges. All is right with the world.

I take these sojourns daily, and so am never far from Him.

In the interim I keep with me always the book of His teachings. Through the word of God one can satisfy the most ardent search for knowledge. Through the good book is opened the way to true wisdom, and therein lies the only road to salvation and eternal happiness.

It is my faith that has carried me through the bloodiest battlefield, that has sustained me through the deaths of thousands of soldiers, and then that of grandchildren and daughters-in-law. Nothing but my faith could have made me accept that the outcome of so bloody a war was yet for the greater good of all.

It is my heart's desire to communicate what burns in me to the world, though I detest public displays. Yet I know many wounds could be salved with a stronger faith in God, a knowledge that there is a grander plan. To those who sorrow for me, those who see me as experiencing most terribly the loss of our freedom, I say: I know you sorrow for us, but you must not be too distressed. We must be resigned to necessity, and commit ourselves in adversity to the will of a merciful God as cheerfully as in prosperity. All is done for our good and our faith must continue unshaken.

These words, bile to some, are like pearls on my tongue. The time for sand is past. I strive for my every act to state that belief loud and clear.

Recently I was graced with the opportunity to demonstrate in no uncertain terms that, although the plan may not yet be revealed to us, we still have a part to play in it. A man of color, previously a stranger to our congregation, went forward to accept communion. Not a soul rose up to follow him, as would have happened had any other parishioner acted similarly.

This man clearly was not welcome, but his faith had prompted him to go forward even amidst the growing hostility. To some, his mere presence in their house of worship was the worst kind of sacrilege, and his audacity in expecting the Eucharist was beyond their ken. Voices lowered piously took on an edge not proper in a place of worship—nor proper anywhere.

I joined the man at the rail, and took my blessing next to him with a glad heart and open mind. Steady faith can sustain a man in even the most trying situation, and I was rewarded when my actions prompted others to follow suit.

Healing is a slow process to be sure, but faith sweetens the medicine.

Though it need not be accompanied by preaching or demand, set not your faith at the doorstep of your office. Invite it inside and allow your trust in God to steady your hand when business dealings trouble you, or your confidence is undermined by failure or defeat. For without faith behind one's desk, no office is complete.

Optimism

I rode out today, among the lands and the people, through the country and on into the city. My eyes saw a wasteland of ruined crops, devastated families, and the blackened, burned shell of what was once a thriving metropolis.

But that is not what my heart saw.

My heart saw—a chance. A chance for a whole generation to start anew, with clean consciences and fresh dreams. A chance for an entire population to experience the freedom that comes with forgiveness. A chance to know the pleasure that comes with doing your best, even if that best did not produce hard-sought results.

Optimism is no easy chore, especially in the bleakest of moments. How should the starving man be happy that he has shoes? If he never finds food, he thinks, even good shoes won't warm the feet of a dead man. And so he is already one step closer to death.

Once I wrote a friend that in the good providence of God, apparent failure often proves a blessing. This I truly believe. Things do happen for a reason, and accepting this allows one to look for the good in all things, easily discounting the bad. And so, instead of marching closer to one's death, one is two steps closer to life.

Attaining such optimism is contingent upon the knowledge that I did my absolute best, that I did my duty to the fullest extent I was able, disregarding all costs and consequences. I will never be free of the knowledge that I failed at the greatest contest ever put to me; my actions led to a horrifying loss of life and property. I did not fulfill the dreams of a nation. My only comfort is that I did my best and in so doing I did my duty. Now I can look at my present situation with a heart that sees the possibilities I've been afforded, even by the same hand that served my earlier failures.

And truly, what good is there in dwelling on the bitterness of loss? What advantage is gained? Best not to think of things at all, rather than expend precious energies on disappointments. Yet the man who does not think, who does not consider and examine his life, is no man at all. Therefore, a man must school himself to the positive, taking note of the negative, but never lingering where naught can be gained.

So, too, be conscious of the fact that your corporate glass is always half full, and never half empty. Thus will you drink of the sweetness of success, even in the face of bitter failure. For what pessimism destroys, yet optimism brings to new life.

EPILOGUE: THE FINAL LESSON

Jase finally closed the back cover of the frayed little book. He was overawed, which was not an accustomed—or comfortable—feeling. With trembling hands that seemed to be someone else's he picked up his drink reflexively, looked at it, and put it down. His food had arrived sometime ago. He hadn't noticed it then, but he dug in now with gusto. It was long cold, yet he didn't care. He'd be home soon.

"I'll surprise the kids and make breakfast tomorrow morning," he mused, feeling much like a distant cousin of Ebenezer Scrooge at the climax of *A Christmas Carol*. "Pancakes, I think. I'll be in the office by nine. I'll take everyone out to lunch to celebrate today's deal. Then I'll really have to knuckle down before that flight Friday morning. That's okay; it's not like I haven't worked late before..."

Jase's mind raced with the now limitless possibilities his life afforded him. His heart was pounding, thumping as if it hadn't beat in months and was trying to make up for lost time. Perhaps it even was.

Jase was actually startled when the seat belt sign flashed overhead; he'd been so busy making plans! The flight attendant came by and, through sheer force of habit, he absently handed her the remains of his meal, as he might a mere servant. As she turned away, something niggled at his soul and forced him to look up at her retreating figure. Clearing his throat unconsciously, he called out to her:

"Ma'am? Pardon me."

Hesitating, she finally turned to face the burly passenger who had been so rude throughout the long evening flight. Barely able to contain her emotions, she grimaced in anticipation of yet another order barked or complaint lodged. "Yes, sir," she forced herself to say.

Jase recognized instantly the face of a wounded soul, and smiled gently to alleviate her fears. "I just," he began, fumbling for the right words that seemed to be buried deep beneath layers of former frustration and indifference. "I just wanted to—thank you." Her surprised smile returned the favor.

Now, too, as if witnessed through someone else's eyes, Jase suddenly noticed the mess he had made in his frantic search for reading material. Why, it seemed like ages ago! He put everything neatly back in its place, all except for the ancient volume bursting with valiant wisdom and sage advice. This he intended to take with him. He couldn't wait to get back to his life, with the little book serving as the glue to hold things together in those dark hours that were sure to come.

Heck, with his business connections and publicity contacts, he could probably approach the publisher of his choice and make a mint out of the tiny volume boasting such large ideas. Perhaps give up these red-eye flights to God knows where—for good.

As the plane landed and taxied to its arrival gate, Jase snapped his briefcase closed and stood with his hidden treasure locked safely inside, patiently waiting for the other first-class passengers to leave the plane. It was refreshing to skip his usual routine: Rush out into the aisle, then tap his fingers on each seat impatiently when the line stopped to let someone else out.

As the last passenger left the compartment Jase stepped into the aisle and then—promptly—stopped. He had the distinct feeling that he'd forgotten something. He turned around, searching the seat and surrounding floor. Finding nothing, he looked over his shoulder toward the exit, but still stood there, irresolute. Something tugged vaguely, but insistently, at the corner of his mind.

Suddenly, the briefcase in his hand, containing the hidden treasure that he'd so recently uncovered, felt heavier than it should ...

Despite the late hour, Jase whistled as he drove home, his top down, his radio off. The drive was an easy one, and it was a heavenly night. When the blinking lights of a plane overhead caught his attention, Jase couldn't help but smile. His briefcase might have been a little lighter when he got off the plane, but his heart was downright weightless.

Somewhere, somehow, another weary traveler searching for reading material in the back of his neighboring seat was about to discover an ancient volume that would shortly change his life. Though Jase had considered absconding with the timeless tome, the lessons he'd learned inside had helped him replace it exactly where he'd found it without fear. After all, he could never forget a single word of its contents. Why should it gather dust on his own crowded bookshelf, or selfishly earn him a profit from making its contents known to the world?

No, better another kindred soul, starved for wisdom, bereft of hope, should stumble upon it as did Jase. It just felt right. As he wound through the deserted highway toward home, Jase smiled. Somehow, he felt, somewhere, perhaps the Last Knight would be smiling as well...

ABOUT THE AUTHOR

Michael Lipsey offers several training products: (1) a ten-volume video training series entitles, Mike Lipsey's Total Real Estate Seminar, providing practical strategies for the effective sale, lease, and management of commercial property, (2) Lipseytv.com, an online, interactive learning format that enables The Lipsey Company to reach and teach more of its clients on a more frequent basis, (3) Visionary Selling for Commercial Real Estate, a 4-volume audio series created in collaboration with best-selling author of Visionary Selling, Barbara Geraghty, and (4) Solutions for Property Managers: Successfully Responding in Changing Times, a 4-volume audio training program with Tom Gille that focuses on practical solutions and customer-focused strategies for property managers.